NEW DIRECTIONS FOR CHILD DEVELOPMENT

William Damon, *Brown University*
EDITOR-IN-CHIEF

Child Care and Maternal Employment: A Social Ecology Approach

Kathleen McCartney
University of New Hampshire

EDITOR

Number 49, Fall 1990

JOSSEY-BASS INC., PUBLISHERS
San Francisco

CHILD CARE AND MATERNAL EMPLOYMENT: A SOCIAL ECOLOGY APPROACH
Kathleen McCartney (ed.)
New Directions for Child Development, no. 49
William Damon, Editor-in-Chief

Microfilm copies of issues and articles are available in 16mm and 35mm, as well as microfiche in 105mm, through University Microfilms Inc., 300 North Zeeb Road, Ann Arbor, Michigan 48106.

LC 85-644581   ISSN 0195-2269   ISBN 1-55542-805-3

NEW DIRECTIONS FOR CHILD DEVELOPMENT is part of The Jossey-Bass Social and Behavioral Science Series and is published quarterly by Jossey-Bass Inc., Publishers (publication number USPS 494-090). Second-class postage paid at San Francisco, California, and at additional mailing offices. Postmaster: Send address changes to Jossey-Bass Inc., Publishers, 350 Sansome Street, San Francisco, California 94104.

EDITORIAL CORRESPONDENCE should be sent to the Editor-in-Chief, William Damon, Department of Education, Box 1938, Brown University, Providence, Rhode Island 02912.

Cover photograph by Wernher Krutein/PHOTOVAULT © 1990.

Printed on acid-free paper in the United States of America.

CONTENTS

EDITOR'S NOTES

Most studies of child care and of maternal employment are natural experiments, that is, they are not really experiments at all. Rather, studies of child care and maternal employment typically compare or match groups instead of experimentally manipulating them. The experimental approach allows a researcher to draw conclusions confidently about the effects of an independent variable on a dependent variable. Unfortunately, this is not the case with natural experiments, though researchers often make bold scientific and policy statements regarding the "effects" of child care and maternal employment.

The effects of any naturally occurring variable, such as child care or maternal employment, are difficult to identify precisely because such variables cannot ordinarily be experimentally manipulated. In general, developmentalists have had to rely on correlational designs to study child care and maternal employment. In correlational designs numerous variables are free to vary and to interact in complex ways.

Even though we learn as undergraduate students that correlation does not imply causality, we want it to be so. Kagan (1979, p. 886) is correct when he accuses modern developmentalists of operating with an obsession to find "absolute principles which declare that a particular set of external conditions is inevitably associated with a fixed set of consequences." In other words, we look for main effects; it is as though we want the laws of development to be simple. However, as Bronfenbrenner (1977, p. 518) has noted, "In ecological research, the principal main effects are likely to be interactions." One assumption of an ecological study of human development is that the laws of development are more likely to be complex than simple.

Using a Social-Ecological Approach to Guide Research

The contributors to this volume have each recognized that natural experiments on any phenomenon must employ a social-ecological approach, such that the developing person is studied in a broader context than the immediate setting of interest, for example, child care. Social-ecological conceptions of development do not constitute theory since there are no testable propositions that derive from them. Rather, such conceptions suggest ways of conducting research, especially natural experiments.

McCartney and Galanopoulos (1988) argue that the effects of child care must be examined with respect to other important social ecologies in the young child's life, especially the family. They argue further that individual differences among developing persons must be considered, for example, differences in age, sex, birth order, and temperament. To examine the effect of child care on any dependent variable one must examine whether identified effects are moderated by aspects of the family context or by aspects of the child. In addition, larger social contexts must be examined. For example, state regulations no doubt have an impact on child care quality.

In order to conduct research, specified ecologies or contexts need to be operationalized. The child care context, for example, could be operationalized with respect to several indicators such as age of entry into care, extensiveness of care, continuity of care, and quality of care. An index such as quality of care could be operationalized by variables such as caregiver-child ratio and caregiver sensitivity. Similarly, the family context needs to be operationalized with respect to variables such as socioeconomic status, family stress and support, and family attitudes, particularly attitudes about maternal employment and child care. Obviously, these two contexts could be operationalized in an infinite number of ways. For this reason, researchers must be guided by theory and by past research when operationalizing any context.

Three Issues for Researchers to Consider

The study of any social structure may very well follow a predictable developmental trajectory, from simple comparisons to a systems-oriented approach. This has been the case with the study of child care and of maternal employment; similarly, this has been the case with the study of school effects (McCartney and Jordan, 1990). The problem is that it is not clear exactly how a social-ecological approach should guide research. It is crucial to note that our conceptions for doing research far exceed our paradigms and our statistics. As developmentalists, we may accept that the developing person exists within various social ecologies, that development is multidetermined, and that relationships between people are transactional; however, we lack the means to model these kinds of complex processes. Nevertheless, we certainly can do more than make simplistic comparisons between two groups of children who vary in their exposure to an immediate setting like child care.

While we await needed methodological advances, we should increase our standards for conducting natural experiments based on a social-ecological model. The contributors to this volume have increased the standards for research on child care through their consideration of three methodological issues.

First, it is likely that there are preexisting differences between any two comparison groups, for example, children in extensive child care versus children cared for exclusively by mothers or children with employed mothers versus children of nonemployed mothers. Although it is clear why research in the field began with these simplistic comparisons, we can no longer make them without serious consideration of other differences that might covary with the use of child care or with maternal employment. In natural experiments preexisting differences that covary with group assignment constitute alternative explanations for identified effects.

There is no reason to expect that families randomly assign their children to child care arrangements. In fact, there is evidence that this is not the case. There is a growing literature that documents associations between family characteristics and use of child care. For example, low-quality care is more likely to be used by low-income families (Howes and Olenick, 1986; Howes and Stewart, 1987; Lamb and others, 1988) and by families with authoritarian educational beliefs (McCartney, 1984). Maternal separation anxiety is associated with the selection of type of child care arrangements (Hock, DeMeis, and McBride, 1987). A number of other variables might reasonably be associated with child care arrangements, perhaps those related to family stress.

Researchers must search for preexisting differences between groups and then consider the consequences of these differences through various data analysis strategies. One strategy is to control statistically for preexisting differences. This strategy was used in the Bermuda Day Care Study through hierarchical multiple regression (McCartney, 1984; Phillips, McCartney, and Scarr, 1987). Another strategy is to examine directly the different social ecologies. Weinraub, Jaeger, and Hoffman (1988) showed that role satisfaction had different correlates for employed versus nonemployed mothers. For employed mothers it was associated with satisfaction with child care help and the ability to cope, while for nonemployed mothers it was associated with satisfaction with emotional supports. A third strategy is to examine family moderators of effects of child care or maternal employment by testing the effects of interactions. In the data from the National Longitudinal Study of Youth, McCartney and Rosenthal (1990) found interactions between maternal employment and family background variables, such as mother's education, when predicting verbal intelligence.

Examinations of preexisting differences among groups are addressed in the four empirical papers presented in this volume. In Chapter One, Jay Belsky and Michael Rovine compare children who had experienced extensive child care with those who had not on eight indicators of family socioeconomic status. In Chapter Four, Susan L. McBride directly studies maternal moderators of child care by examining associations between maternal separation anxiety and maternal employment patterns. In Chapter Two by Deborah Lowe Vandell and Mary Ann Corasaniti and in Chapter Three by Ricardo C. Ainslie, indicators of the family and child care contexts are examined in the same analysis.

The second issue for researchers to consider is that measures must be examined in an ecological context. Several recent studies suggest that extensive child care during the first year of life may disrupt mother-child attachment (for example, Belsky and Rovine, 1988; Barglow, Vaughn, and Molitor, 1987). Attachment has traditionally been measured with the Strange Situation Assessment, which is a laboratory paradigm that consists of a series of separations and reunions between a baby and the baby's mother and a stranger. Children with extensive child care appear avoidant during reunions with their mothers. Clarke-Stewart and Fein (1983) have questioned whether the Strange Situation is a valid measure for children with extensive child care who experience daily separations and reunions with their parents. It is possible that this measure is not valid for all children in all contexts. The need for validation studies of such measures is crucial.

In this volume, Belsky and Rovine address the issue of whether the Strange Situation is a valid measure of attachment by including a second measure of attachment, the Attachment Q-Sort (Waters and Deane, 1985), in their study. Theirs is the only study of child care and attachment that has included multiple measures of attachment. Because their results do not replicate across instruments, this study confirms the need for validation studies of measures.

The third issue is familiar to developmentalists, namely, the need for longitudinal studies of child care and maternal employment. There may be important mediators of effects that can only be identified through longitudinal study. The National Institute of Child Health and Human Development is currently conducting a ten-site longitudinal study of twelve hundred children, their families, and their child care providers. Large-scale, longitudinal, collaborative studies like this will lead to the greatest gains in knowledge and represent the way that research will most likely be conducted in the future.

There are few longitudinal studies of child care or of maternal employment. In this volume, Vandell and Corasaniti present the results of a retrospective study that documents pervasive differences among third graders as a function of infant child care. They discuss their findings in terms of a particular context, namely, that the study was conducted in a state with minimal child care standards, at a time of pronounced confounding of family and child care factors. In fact, child outcomes were best predicted by a combination of child care and family variables. The disturbing results of this retrospective study will help guide future longitudinal studies.

In addition, experimental studies of child care, and possibly of maternal employment, can be and should be conducted. Bronfenbrenner (1977, p. 518) writes, "If you wish to understand the relation between the developing person and some aspect of his or her environment, try to budge the one, and see what happens to the other." Various interventions are possible, as best exemplified by the Carolina Abecedarian Project, in which poverty-stricken children were randomly assigned to a high-quality day-care center as a form of early childhood intervention (Ramey and Campbell, 1987).

Such experiments are likely to be costly in that they involve the manipulation of real-life environments; however, Bronfenbrenner is no doubt correct that we need to "disturb the existing balance" between person and environment to understand it fully.

Contribution of This Volume

The first four chapters in this volume are empirical papers that represent the state-of-the-art in research on child care and maternal employment, in that child development is considered in a broad context. The volume concludes with Chapter Five, a conceptual paper by Elizabeth Jaeger and Marsha Weinraub, in which they describe fundamental theoretical differences among child care and maternal employment researchers; their paper offers a needed bridge between these two overlapping areas of research.

This volume makes three contributions. First, the concepts utilized all direct the field toward a social-ecological conception of child care and maternal employment, specifically, and of child development, generally. Second, the empirical approaches advanced serve as models for how research on child care and maternal employment should be conducted. Third, the findings presented will guide future research on and social policy for children.

In closing, I gratefully acknowledge the editorial assistance of Amanda Diggins and Saul Rosenthal in the preparation of this volume. This project was supported, in part, by a grant from the National Institute of Child Health and Human Development (U10-HD25451-01) and a grant from the National Institute of Mental Health (R01-MH43879-01). I also acknowledge the support of the Whitcomb Professorship.

Kathleen McCartney
Editor

References

Barglow, P., Vaughn, B. E., and Molitor, N. "Effects of Maternal Absence Due to Employment on the Quality of Infant-Mother Attachment in a Low-Risk Sample." *Child Development*, 1987, *58*, 945–954.

Belsky, J., and Rovine, M. J. "Nonmaternal Care in the First Year of Life and the Security of Infant-Parent Attachment." *Child Development*, 1988, *49*, 157–167.

Bronfenbrenner, U. "Toward an Experimental Ecology of Human Development." *American Psychologist*, 1977, *32*, 513–531.

Clarke-Stewart, K. A., and Fein, G. C. "Early Childhood Programs." In M. Haith and J. Campos (eds.), *Handbook of Child Psychology*. Vol. 2: *Infancy and Developmental Psychobiology*. (4th ed.) New York: Wiley, 1983.

Hock, E., DeMeis, D., and McBride, S. "Maternal Separation Anxiety: Its Role in the Balance of Employment and Motherhood in Mothers and Infants." In A. E. Gottfried and A. W. Gottfried (eds.), *Maternal Employment and Children's Development: Longitudinal Research*. New York: Plenum, 1988.

Howes, C., and Olenick, M. "Family and Child Care Influences on Toddlers' Compliance." *Child Development,* 1986, *57,* 202–216.

Howes, C., and Stewart, P. "Child's Play with Adults, Toys, and Peers: An Examination of Family and Child-Care Influence." *Developmental Psychology,* 1987, *23,* 423–430.

Kagan, J. "Family Experience and the Child's Development." *American Psychologist,* 1979, *34,* 886–891.

Lamb, M., Hwang, C., Bookstein, F. L., Broberg, A., Hult, G., and Frodi, M. "Determinants of Social Competence in Swedish Preschoolers." *Developmental Psychology,* 1988, *24,* 58–70.

McCartney, K. "Effect of Quality of Day Care Environment on Children's Language Development." *Child Development,* 1984, *20,* 244–260.

McCartney, K., and Galanopoulos, A. "Childcare and Attachment: A New Frontier the Second Time Around." *American Journal of Orthopsychiatry,* 1988, *58,* 16–24.

McCartney, K., and Jordan, E. "Parallels Between Research on Child Care and Research on School Effects." *Educational Researcher,* 1990, *19,* 21–27.

McCartney, K., and Rosenthal, S. R. "Moderators of Maternal Employment Effects on Children's Adjustment." Paper presented at the International Conference on Infancy Studies, Montreal, Canada, April 20, 1990.

Phillips, D., McCartney, K., and Scarr, S. "Child-Care Quality and Children's Social Development." *Developmental Psychology,* 1987, *23,* 537–543.

Ramey, C. T., and Campbell, F. A. "The Carolina Abecedarian Project: An Educational Experiment." In J. J. Gallagher and C. T. Ramey (eds.), *The Malleability of Children.* Baltimore, Md.: Brookes, 1987.

Waters, E., and Deane, K. E. "Defining and Assessing Individual Differences in Attachment Relationships: Q-Methodology and the Organization of Behavior in Infancy and Early Childhood." In I. Bretherton and E. Waters (eds.), *Growing Points of Attachment Theory and Research.* Monographs of the Society for Research in Child Development, vol. 50, nos. 1–2 (serial 209). Chicago: University of Chicago Press, 1985.

Weinraub, M., Jaeger, E., and Hoffman, L. "Predicting Infant Outcome in Families of Employed and Non-Employed Mothers." *Early Childhood Research Quarterly,* 1988, *3,* 361–378.

Kathleen McCartney is an associate professor of psychology at the University of New Hampshire, Durham.

Can a Q-Sort measure of attachment security take the place of a Strange Situation Assessment to study infant day care? Apparently not, but it can be used in conjunction with the more traditional measurement strategy.

Q-Sort Security and First-Year Nonmaternal Care

Jay Belsky, Michael Rovine

Close scrutiny of research pertaining to the development of children reared by persons other than their parents led the first author, in 1986, to argue that sufficient evidence existed to conclude that extensive nonparental care initiated in the first year of life was a "risk factor" for the development of insecure infant-parent attachments and subsequent noncompliance and aggression among three-to-eight-year-olds (Belsky, 1986). Although it has been popular to criticize this argument on the basis of potential problems with the primary methodology used to assess infant-parent attachment security, namely, the Ainsworth and Wittig (1969) Strange Situation (Clarke-Stewart, 1988, 1989; Phillips, McCartney, Scarr, and Howes, 1987; Thompson, 1988), three points in defense of the original reasoning are rarely acknowledged.

First, central to the analysis of the developmental correlates of extensive infant day-care experience was the understanding that processes of influence were difficult, if not impossible, to discern at the time and thus that it remained unclear whether day-care experience, separation of infant from parent, family processes, or some combination of these forces was responsible for the disconcerting evidence presented. It was for this very reason that the phrase "ecology of infant day care" was used.

Second, by employing the term "risk factor," an effort was made to highlight the probabilistic, rather than inevitable, nature of the association between extensive nonparental care experience in the first year and patterns of development that could be regarded as troubling. In particular, this terminology was selected to highlight the fact that the risks associated with infant day care were most likely to be realized in interaction with other

NEW DIRECTIONS FOR CHILD DEVELOPMENT, no. 49, Fall 1990 © Jossey-Bass Inc., Publishers sources of risk, whether emanating from the child, the family, or the child care situation itself. In retrospect it is evident that many who read the essay were not familiar with risk-factor terminology and its routine usage in the fields of epidemiology and developmental psychopathology from which it was borrowed. As a result, the essay was interpreted as implying more determinism than ever intended.

Third, and perhaps the most important feature of the Belsky (1986) analysis, it was not the attachment data per se that led to the conclusion that extensive infant day care was a "risk factor." Rather, it was the combination of three independent sets of evidence, one linking extensive infant day care with elevated rates of insecurity, another linking similar care experience with increased levels of aggression and noncompliance, and a third, totally unconcerned with issues of day care, indicating, in line with propositions derived from attachment theory, that increased aggression and noncompliance were related to insecure patterns of infant-parent attachment in samples of mostly traditionally reared children (Belsky, 1988). If the only evidence available had been data linking insecure attachment with day-care experience, the point of view articulated in the essay would never have been advanced by its author.

In the time since the writing of the 1986 essay, three pieces of evidence have been reported to strengthen the conviction that, in the main, there is something of concern going on in the ecology of infant day care as it is routinely experienced in the United States today. First, our own research on families going through the transition to parenthood reveals, like other studies cited in the 1986 essay, that extensive nonparental care initiated in the first year is associated with elevated rates of insecure infant-parent attachment security (Belsky and Rovine, 1988). Second, Vandell and Corasaniti's (this issue) data indicate that among a large sample of third graders from middle-class families in the Dallas area, those exposed to the kind of nonparental care routinely available to such families for more than thirty hours per week beginning in their first year of life were among the most poorly scoring children on a variety of indices of academic and social adjustment, including teacher and parent ratings of compliance, peer ratings of likability, personal ratings of self-esteem, achievement test performance, and conduct grades.

A third important investigation was conducted by Howes (1990), which reveals in a manner totally consistent with a risk-factor model that children who began nonparental care on a full-time basis in their first year and who were receiving poor-quality care by the time they were eighteen months of age, evinced more socioemotional difficulty than children whose care began after the first year, whether of high or low quality, or whose care began within the first year but was of high quality subsequently. Thus, age of entry and extent of care, even in the face of considerations of quality of care, emerged as an important set of predictors of social development when dependent variables were measured in the second, third, and fourth years of life.

Rather than refuting the assertion that extensive nonparental care initiated in the first year is a risk factor in the development of insecure infant-parent attachment, noncompliance, and aggression, then, the results of these recent studies provide additional support for it. The point to be made, though, is not that extensive nonparental care in the first year poses an inevitable developmental risk for the child or that we know why these disconcerting associations obtain. Rather, the point is that when it comes to understanding the complex ecology of day care, issues pertaining to age of entry and extent of care must be considered along with those of quality, stability, and reasons for and parental feelings about care utilization.

Perhaps the best evidence that infant day care, under the right conditions, need not pose a developmental risk is in a fourth investigation that has appeared since the publication of Belsky (1986). In this study of Swedish children reared since infancy in day care, Andersson (1989) found that no deficits at age eight could be linked with early day-care entry, and that, in fact, some developmental advantages were associated with full-time nonparental care initiated in the first year. To understand why these data are so dramatically at odds with those cited above, particularly those from comparably aged children in the Vandell and Corasaniti (this issue) research, just consider the facts that all the parents of the children in the Swedish study received paid parental leave from their jobs until their infants were six months of age and then were able to place their babies in centers staffed by well-trained and reasonably well-paid caregivers. There is no indication that such childrearing and family conditions obtained except on an exceptional basis for children in the other studies.

In other words, as evidence continues to accumulate and raise concerns about developmental risks associated with extensive nonparental care initiated in the first year of life, as it is routinely experienced in this country, and as calls are being made for additional research to illuminate the conditions under which and the processes by which extensive infant day care does and does not pose developmental risks, cross-cultural evidence convincingly demonstrates that public policies can foster conditions that promote rather than undermine the development of infants cared for on a full-time basis by persons other than their parents. Clearly, there are grounds for rapprochement between those who emphasize age of entry and extent of care (Belsky, 1986, 1988) and those who underscore quality of care (Phillips, McCartney, Scarr, and Howes, 1987). Simply put, we need to attend to a host of child care conditions, including age of entry and extent of care (Belsky, in press).

Alternatives to the Strange Situation

As alluded to above, of foremost importance to those who doubt the presence of risks associated with infant day care are questions about the validity of the Strange Situation paradigm in the comparative study of children with and without extensive day-care experience. The argument advanced repeatedly is that since day-care-reared children are more familiar with such separations than more traditionally reared children, the two groups of children differentially experience the Strange Situation and the separations purposefully designed into it, thereby rendering problematical all comparisons using this methodology (Clarke-Stewart, 1988, 1989; Phillips, McCartney, Scarr, and Howes, 1987; Thompson, 1988). Although it is impossible at the present time to draw firm conclusions with regard to this scientifically plausible but (to date) empirically unsubstantiated hypothesis, elsewhere we have summarized a wealth of data that are inconsistent with the proposition that the elevated rates of insecurity associated with extensive experience of nonparental care in the first year, when measured using the Strange Situation, are an artifact of the assessment system (Belsky, 1989). Our purpose in this chapter is not to reiterate points made elsewhere but rather to consider an alternative approach to the assessment of attachment security with regard to issues surrounding infant day care.

In response to concerns raised about the validity of the Strange Situation Assessment, Waters and Deane (1985) developed an alternative method of assessing attachment security, one that requires extensive observation of infants under naturalistic conditions in their homes before describing their most characteristic and least characteristic behaviors (related to attachment) by means of a list of one hundred behaviorally descriptive statements. Their Attachment Q-Sort is regarded by many as a viable alternative methodology and, especially in the case of day-care research, is considered particularly valid since it does not require that children be subjected to separations. As a possible alternative methodology, several questions arise, all of which are addressed in this report. First, does attachment security measured using the Q-Sort covary with attachment security assessed by the more traditional Strange Situation? That is, is there any evidence of concurrent validity? Second, if evidence of such validity exists, is the Q-Sort sensitive to variation in infant day-care experience? If it is not, some researchers are ready to conclude that results emanating from studies using the Strange Situation are indeed an artifact of the separation-based methodology (Clarke-Stewart, 1989).

Finally, and perhaps most important, can the Q-Sort be used to advance the study of the ecology of infant day care? Weinraub, Jaeger, and Hoffman (1988) recently presented data suggesting that the correlates of Q-Sort security are distinctly different across samples of children with and without extensive nonparental care experience. Most noteworthy is their finding that while security and dependency (also measured via the Q-Sort) were significantly negatively correlated in the case of eighteen-month-olds with full-time working mothers ($r = -.71$, $p < .01$), the same association was positive and marginally significant in the case of children whose mothers did not work ($r = .42$, $p < .10$), resulting in a highly significant difference between the two correlation coefficients ($z = 3.27$, $p < .001$). To the extent this is a replicable finding, it may be one of the most important discerned to date, as it suggests not simply that levels of functioning differ within children growing up in different family and child care ecologies but that the dynamics of psychological development may be different as well.

Because the samples used in the Weinraub, Jaeger, and Hoffman study were so small ($N = 15$ in each group), it is important to be cautious about the meaning of their data. Using a substantially larger sample drawn from our longitudinal studies and reported on elsewhere with regard to infant day care and the Strange Situation (Belsky and Rovine, 1988), we determined the replicability of the most provocative and potentially significant results of the Weinraub, Jaeger, and Hoffman study. We also attempted to see whether attachment security as measured by Q-Sort is differentially related to maternal, child, and family factors in samples of children that vary in their exposure to routine nonmaternal care.

Methods. *Subjects.* Subjects of the replication investigation were ninety-four first-born infants (sixty-one boys, thirty-three girls) and their mothers who participated in the third cohort of the Pennsylvania Infant and Family Development Project. There are more boys than girls in the sample because, despite prenatal enrollment of families, more boys were born to participating families. All families were maritally intact and were enrolled in a longitudinal study during the last trimester of pregnancy.

Design. Information regarding parents' employment and child-care arrangements was obtained during the course of interviews with parents conducted when infants were three, nine, and twelve months of age. For purposes of this study, this information was used to identify two groups of children that varied as a function of nonmaternal care experience: (1) those who averaged twenty or more hours per week of infant day care ($N = 34$) and (2) those who averaged less time, including none at all ($N = 60$). This grouping was chosen because sample size limited utilization of the four-group design used in a previous report in which the focus was on Strange Situation classifications, and because that inquiry (Belsky and Rovine, 1988), like others, highlighted the importance of extensive care experience (for example, Barglow, Vaughn, and Molitor, 1987; Jacobson and Wille, 1984).

Actual care arrangements utilized by families varied a great deal and included father care, other relative care, in-home babysitter care, group care, and family day care. Because data for this investigation were obtained as part of a larger study of infant and family development, limited resources precluded collection of detailed information on the child care placement itself. Although this design feature severely limited our ability to address empirically several important issues, particularly those pertaining to quality of care, it assured that families participating in the study had no reason to believe that the larger project was particularly concerned about issues of day care and maternal employment. Analyses of the results of other investigations strongly suggest that such knowledge of study purposes can affect who participates in research and the results that obtain vis-à-vis infant day care (Belsky, 1988; Belsky and Rovine, 1988).

Attachment Assessments. Two methods of assessing infant-mother attachment security were employed when infants were one year of age. As reported in an earlier paper (Belsky and Rovine, 1988), infants were videotaped in the Strange Situation, a laboratory procedure that subjects the infant to repeated separations and reunions with mother and an adult female stranger for purposes of creating stress and evoking attachment behaviors (for example, seeking contact and proximity). On the basis of standardized classification techniques, infant-parent relationships were judged to be secure (B), insecure-avoidant (A), or insecure-resistant (C). All tapes were coded by at least two independent coders, each of whom had achieved 90 percent reliability with an experienced evaluator. In addition to overall security classifications, interactive ratings of avoidance and of resistance directed toward mothers during the two reunion episodes were available for analysis.

At the completion of the Strange Situation Assessment, mothers were given a list of one hundred statements from Waters and Deane's (1985) Attachment Q-Sort describing infant-toddler attachment behavior. The manner of eventually sorting these statements for purposes of characterizing their infants was outlined to them, and they were instructed to read over the statements several times to become familiar with them and then pay attention to these behaviors of their children during the following week. One week later mothers received one hundred slips of paper in the mail, each with one of the statements printed on it. They were asked to sort these statements into nine piles (with equal numbers of items) ranging from "most characteristic" of their children to "least characteristic" of their children and to return their sortings to the research project office by mail.

These sortings were used to generate four scores by correlating the mothers' item placements (in one of the nine piles) with those of the "expert" sorters from whom Waters and Deane obtained criterion sorts for each of the four dimensions that the Q-Sort was designed to measure: security, sociability, dependency, and social desirability. This procedure resulted in each child receiving four scores in the form of correlation coefficients (ranging from −1.00 to 1.00) that reflected the extent to which each mother's behavioral description of her child characterized the child as secure, dependent, and sociable, and herself as a provider of socially desirable responses.

Results. Five sets of analyses were conducted. In a series of preliminary analyses, comparisons were made between child care groups to determine whether families using extensive care versus those not using such care differed with respect to demographic factors even before their babies were born. The second set of analyses was designed to determine whether Q-Sort measures covaried with respect to the attachment security classifications obtained on the basis of observations of infant behavior in the Strange Situation. The third set of analyses sought to determine whether security as measured by the Attachment Q-Sort varied as a function of child care experience in the first year of life. The fourth set of analyses was designed to determine whether the dynamics of psychological development, as indexed by the intercorrelation of Q-Sort subscores, varied as a function of child care experience. Finally, the fifth set of analyses was designed to determine whether social-ecological correlates of Q-Sort security (that is, characteristics of mother, infant, and family) were similar or different for the two groups of subjects.

Preliminary Analyses: Background Comparisons. Comparison of the two groups of infants on eight demographic measures (involving prenatal family income and age, education, and occupation of each husband and wife) taken during the prenatal interviews revealed that families that relied on extensive nonmaternal care during their infants' first year of life had larger incomes [Ms = \$28,850 versus \$23,340, t (92) = 2.07, $p < .05$] and the fathers had somewhat fewer years of schooling [Ms = 15.82 versus 16.90, t (92) = 1.64, $p < .10$], though both groups were relatively well educated. (Income data were gathered only for each family as a whole, not for each parent individually.) Because none of these potentially confounding variables was significantly correlated with any of the indices of child psychological functioning obtained from the Q-Sort (see Table 4), either for the total sample or within either group, these preexisting group differences were not statistically controlled in subsequent analyses.

Strange Situation and Q-Sort: Concurrent Validity. Two forms of Q-Sort measures were available for analysis in order to address the issue of the interrelation of Q-Sort scores and Strange Situation classifications. In addition to the simple Q-Sort scores generated by the correlation between each mother's sort and the expert criterion sort, correlations adjusted (via partial correlation analysis) for social desirability were also available (because of the high correlation between Q-security and Q-social desirability: $r = .85$). Because it was difficult to determine which representation of Q-Sort reports was most valid, both were subjected to a three-group (A, B, C) one-way analysis of variance, with follow-up testing to assess the significance of differences between infants classified as secure (B) and those classified as insecure (A + C) in the Strange Situation. The results of these analyses are displayed in Table 1.

Table 1. Adjusted and Unadjusted (for Social Desirability) Q-Sort Scores as a Function of Strange Situation Classification

	Strange Situation Classification				Secure (B) versus Insecure (A + C)
	Insecure Avoidant (A)	Secure (B)	Insecure Resistant (C)	F	
	(N = 13)	(N = 68)	(N = 14)	(2, 92)	(1, 93)
Unadjusted					
Security	.60	.59	.56	ns	ns
Dependency	-.10	-.04	-.02	ns	ns
Sociability	.57	.56	.55	ns	ns
Adjusted					
Security	.09	.23	.16	6.82[b]	11.90[c]
Dependency	.02	.16	.18	4.11[a]	ns
Sociability	.05	.16	.15	4.05[a]	4.41[a]

Note: ns = nonsignificant

[a] $p < .05$
[b] $p < .01$
[c] $p < .001$

Inspection of the table reveals that only levels of Q-Sort scores adjusted for social desirability differ significantly according to Strange Situation classifications. Children classified secure in the Strange Situation evinced more security at home according to their mothers than those classified insecure, with children classified as insecure-avoidant receiving the lowest adjusted Q-security scores from a correlational perspective. This differential sensitivity of adjusted and unadjusted Q-security scores is reflected in the associations between Strange Situation classification (A = insecure, C = insecure, B = secure) and adjusted Q-security ($r = .31$, $p < .005$) and unadjusted Q-security ($r = .03$, ns).

Differences across the three attachment groups also emerged in the cases of dependency and sociability. And while secure infants receive higher sociability scores than all insecure infants using the Q-Sort measure, inspection of the means reveals that this effect is a function of the low-sociability scores of insecure-avoidant infants. Indeed, when tests were carried out comparing insecure-avoidant infants with all others, significant differences emerged, indicating that infants classified in the Strange Situation as insecure-avoidant in their attachments to their mothers were regarded by their mothers (after adjusting for social desirability) as less dependent and less sociable than other infants [$F (1, 93) = 7.82$, $p < .01$; 6, 70, $p < .05$, respectively].

Q-Security and Nonmaternal Care. In light of these findings it was deemed appropriate to address the issue of nonmaternal care and Q-security, dependency, and sociability using only the adjusted scores. This was done by subjecting the adjusted Q-scores to a 2 (Group) × 2 (Gender) analysis of variance. Results of this analysis, presented in Table 2, reveal only a marginal difference between the child care groups in the case of the Q-security score and no main or interaction effects involving gender. Consistent with results from our prior analysis using Strange Situation classifications (Belsky and Rovine, 1988), the adjusted Q-security data indicated that children who experienced extensive nonmaternal care in their first year looked less secure than those who experienced less than twenty hours per week of such care (effect size: $\Delta = 2.77$). Note that although the interaction of gender and nonmaternal care status did not prove to be significant, boys with extensive care experience had the lowest (adjusted) security mean (.14), with girls with extensive care (.20) scoring almost as highly as boys (.21) and girls (.24) with limited care experience.

To follow up these results, an additional analysis was undertaken in hopes of taking advantage of the well-documented benefits of aggregating indicators of a construct to increase measurement reliability and thereby empirical sensitivity (Epstein, 1979; Rushton, Brainerd, and Pressley, 1983). Specifically, four indicators of attachment security were combined to create an aggregate composite index of insecurity, which was then analyzed. To create the aggregate insecurity index, scores on total avoidance and resistance directed toward mothers in the Strange Situation were summed together, and subtracted from this total was the adjusted Q-security score and a rating of the degree to which the Strange Situation subclassifications deviated from what is considered to be the prototypical manifestation of security, the B3 subclassification (A1/C2 = 1, A2/C1 = 2, B4 = 3, B1/B2 = 5, B3 = 6). The subclassifications of the A-B-C categories reflect differences in separation and reunion behavior. Specifically, secure infants classified as B3 greet their mothers following separation and return to play after being comforted. Secure infants classified as B1 and B2 display some distress upon separation but greet their mothers unambiguously upon reunion. In contrast, infants classified B4 are very upset at separation and seek comfort from their mothers such that they are often hesitant to return fully

Table 2. Adjusted Q-Sort Scores as a Function of Nonmaternal Care

Q-Scores	Extensive Care (N = 34)	Limited Care (N = 60)	F		
			Care (1, 90)	Sex (1, 90)	Care × Sex (1, 90)
Security	.17	.22	2.78[a]	ns	ns
Sociability	.14	.15	ns	ns	ns
Dependency	.15	.14	ns	ns	ns

Note: ns = nonsignificant

[a] $p < .10$

to play. Insecure infants classified as A2 and C1 show moderate levels of avoidance and resistance, respectively, whereas those classified as A1 and C2 evince the most avoidance and resistance, respectively. Thus, the composite index used here includes three distinct types of data: interactive ratings of behavior observed in the Strange Situation, appraisals of security based, in part, on these ratings, and an index of security based on maternal Q-Sort (that is, avoid + resist - Q-security - B3 deviation).

Consistent with the trend in the Q-security analysis, results revealed that infants with more than twenty hours of nonmaternal care experience in their first year evinced significantly more insecurity on the composite index than did infants with extensive day care-experience in their first year [$Ms = 5.83$ versus 2.19, $F (1, 83) = 4.50$, $p < .01$]. In fact, when this insecurity index was examined as a function of a more refined scaling of extent of nonmaternal care, it was discovered that infants who experienced more than thirty-five hours per week of care averaged the highest score (6.69), those with twenty to thirty-five hours per week of care the next highest (4.19), those with ten to twenty hours per week of care the second lowest (2.39), and those with less than ten hours per week of care the lowest (2.12). In other words, there existed a rather orderly relation between extent of nonmaternal care in the first year and degree of insecurity as measured by the multimethod aggregate insecurity score.

Interrelation of Q-Sort Scores by Child Care Group. The fourth analysis undertaken represented an attempt to replicate Weinraub, Jaeger, and Hoffman's (1988) finding that Q-security and Q-dependency are differentially correlated in the case of children who vary in their exposure to extensive nonmaternal care. Recall that the association found by Weinraub, Jaeger, and Hoffman, using a seventy-five-item Q-Sort scale (rather than our one-hundred-item set), was negative in the case of children whose mothers worked full-time and positive in the case of mothers who were not employed. In our sample, the correlation between adjusted Q-security and adjusted Q-dependency was positive, significant, and virtually identical in the cases of children who averaged more than twenty hours and less than twenty hours per week of nonmaternal care in their first year (see Table 3). When the analysis was restricted, as in Weinraub, Jaeger, and Hoffman's study, to just those children whose mothers worked either full time (more than thirty-five hours per week) or not at all, roughly similar positive correlations also emerged [$r (24) = .46$, $p < .001$ versus $r (42) = .67$, $p < .001$]. Even though these findings pertain to correlations between Q-security and Q-dependency scores with each adjusted for social desirability, it is noteworthy that when the analyses just reported were repeated without controlling for social desirability, the interrelation of Q-security and Q-dependency was still similar in the two groups. In other words, in this analysis of a much larger sample, using a larger Q-set, we failed to replicate Weinraub, Jaeger, and Hoffman's provocative finding suggesting that the

Table 3. Intercorrelation of Adjusted Q-Sort Scores in
Two Subsamples with Varying Child Care Experiences

| | Extensive Care | | Limited Care | |
	Security	Dependency	Security	Dependency
Dependency	.60[a]		.62[a]	
Sociability	.20	.52[a]	.19	.42[a]

[a] $p < .001$

dynamics of development with regard to attachment security differ across children with varying child care experience in their first year of life. Furthermore, as the data displayed in Table 3 indicate, this was also true of the interrelation of security and sociability, and of sociability and dependency in the two subsamples.

Social-Ecological Correlates of Q-Security by Child Care Group. Weinraub, Jaeger, and Hoffman (1988) also reported in their small sample study that external correlates of attachment security, as indexed by Q-sort scores, varied by maternal employment and thus child care experience. This led them to assert that "different variables in the family system are predictive of optimal socio-emotional outcomes for children of employed and children of nonemployed mothers" (1988, p. 376).

In attempting to further explore this issue, a series of measures obtained during the course of the longitudinal research, of which the study of infant day-care experience was only a small part, were correlated with adjusted Q-security scores. These measures included the demographic variables mentioned earlier, prenatal assessments of positive and negative marital activities and sentiments (see Belsky, Rovine, and Fish, 1989) and maternal personality (Belsky and Isabella, 1988), three-month maternal reports of infant temperament (Belsky and Rovine, 1987), and nine-month reports of the mothers' desire to work either more or less than they were at time of assessment (Belsky and Rovine, 1988). As can be seen in Table 4, these variables were virtually unrelated to Q-security in either group, and the resultant correlations showed no pattern of differential association as a function of child-care and maternal-employment experience.

Discussion

Concerns raised recently about developmental risks associated with extensive nonparental care initiated in the first year of life have been the subject of widespread criticism. Two issues in particular merit consideration, one of which seems extremely well founded and the other of which is regarded as suspect.

Because only a single study that raises concern has involved random assignment (Haskins, 1985), there are sound reasons to wonder whether

**Table 4. Intercorrelation of (Adjusted) Q-Security and
External Social-Ecological Variables by Child Care Group**

	Extensive Care	Limited Care
Demographic Variables		
Prenatal income	.06	.17
Husband age	.18	-.01
Wife age	.23	.20
Years married	-.04	-.03
Husband education	.10	.14
Wife education	.05	.13
Husband occupation	-.09	.04
Wife occupation	-.03	-.18
Prenatal Marriage		
Positive activities and sentiments	.22	.09
Negative activities and sentiments	-.21	-.07
Mother Personality		
Ego strength	.16	.04
Self-esteem	.10	.05
Interpersonal affect	-.10	-.09
Three-Months Temperament		
Fussy difficult	.04	.00
Dull	-.18	-.19
Unpredictable	.11	.04
Unadaptable	.10	.00
Nine-Months Work Preference		
Desire to work more	-.23	-.13
Desire to work less	.19	.08

the insecurity, noncompliance, and aggression correlates of extensive non-parental care initiated in the first year are a function of day-care experience per se or of some third variable. Quite conceivably, it is the families that chose to rely on such care, rather than the care itself, that are responsible for the findings that led Belsky (1986, 1988) to view extensive infant day care as a "risk factor" (Clarke-Stewart, 1988; Phillips, McCartney, Scarr, and Howes, 1987). Until more work is done that controls for preexisting differences between families that do and do not use day care—and not just differences on demographic indices as in this inquiry—it remains impossible to determine the exact source of the risk that has been highlighted.

A second issue that has been raised by critics of Belsky's analysis centers on the Strange Situation methodology for measuring attachment security. Recall from the introduction that because this procedure is heavily dependent on separation of infant from mother, some researchers have argued that the elevated rates of insecurity associated with extensive non-parental care in the first year of life may be an artifact of children's differential exposure to separation as a result of their varying day-care experience. In particular, an argument has been made that infants with day-care experience will be less stressed by separation because they are more familiar with it and that their tendency to maintain distance has been misconstrued as avoidance, thereby resulting in faulty judgments of insecurity (Clarke-Stewart, 1988; Thompson, 1988).

In response to these challenges to the validity of the Strange Situation as a measure of attachment security, calls have been made for the development and utilization of alternative methods that do not depend so heavily on infants' and toddlers' responses to separation (Clarke-Stewart 1988; Thompson, 1988). Fortunately, we collected Attachment Q-Sorts as part of our longitudinal study. In this chapter we have sought to determine whether Q-Sorts completed by mothers generate scores on psychologically important constructs that can be validated with respect to the Strange Situation, and whether such scores are also sensitive to variation in nonparental care experience. The fact that only scores adjusted for social desirability covary significantly with Strange Situation classifications underscores the need to distinguish between raw scores and adjusted scores. Before we feel entirely confident that only adjusted scores are valid, however, we want to see our findings replicated. In view of them, though, it seemed only appropriate to pursue the issue of child care history using adjusted scores.

When this was done, evidence consistent with Strange Situation findings emerged, though not as strongly as was the case with formal attachment classifications. Recall that the difference between infants with and without extensive day-care experience, though in the direction anticipated, only qualified as a trend ($p < .10$). It is worth noting, however, that had we cast the test as a directional hypothesis, as justified in view of other evidence in the literature, and carried out a one-tailed test of significance, the difference would have achieved conventional levels ($p < .05$). Perhaps more important, though, is how the Q-security score performed when conceptualized not as a stand-alone indicator but rather as one part of a multiple-indicator composite. When this composite index was analyzed, it proved more sensitive to variation in child care history than when the Q-Sort measure (or the other composite components) was examined by itself. Indeed, not only did the composite insecurity index reveal a rather orderly relation between extent of nonmaternal care in the first year and degree of insecurity, but also the inclusion of the Q-security component in the composite increased the sensitivity of the composite to variation in child care experience beyond what it was before the Q-security component was included.

These findings lead to the conclusion that the (adjusted) Q-security index is best employed as one of several indicators of security rather than as a sensitive index all by itself. At present, then, if a choice has to be made between the Strange Situation and the Q-Sort, we recommend the former measure. In a study area in which there may be too great a willingness to embrace null findings, serious limits on discovery seem to exist by virtue of sole reliance on a measurement system that to date does not evince the sensitivity of the Strange Situation.

Further support for this conclusion is in the results of our correlational analyses linking Q-security with external social-ecological variables. The fact that none of these potential correlates proved to be significantly related to Q-security was surprising since in our other work dealing with infant day care in particular (Belsky and Rovine, 1988) and with infant and family development in general (for example, Belsky, Rovine, and Fish, 1989; Belsky and Isabella, 1988; Belsky and Rovine, 1987), these measures covaried in theoretically meaningful ways with attachment security as indexed by Strange Situation classifications. On the basis of the Q-security data alone, one might be led to embrace the null hypothesis and conclude that conditions of elevated risk of insecurity above and beyond extensive infant day-care experience are not identifiable in this study; yet data reported by Belsky and Rovine (1988) as well as by others (Ainslie, 1987; Benn, 1986; see Belsky, 1989, for review) clearly demonstrate that significant differences are found when the Strange Situation is used to assess attachment security.

The final issue that the current report was designed to address involved the replication of Weinraub, Jaeger, and Hoffman's (1988) provocative finding suggesting that the dynamics of psychological development, in particular the interrelation of security and dependency, are different in the cases of infants with and without extensive nonmaternal care experience. With a sample size far larger than the fifteen children per group that Weinraub, Jaeger, and Hoffman used, no evidence of differential associations was obtained in the present inquiry, thereby alerting us to the risks of prematurely embracing provocative and unreplicated findings. Indeed, replication should be required before conclusions are drawn anytime evidence entails different patterns of correlations in different groups that are not anticipated on theoretical grounds in advance of their documentation. The risk of reading meaning into what are likely to be chance findings seems too great to permit sporadic evidence to be turned into meaningful findings, as some seem inclined to do (Clarke-Stewart, 1989).

In sum, while there is a strong desire to advance the state of research on infant day care, there are real risks associated with abandoning well-established procedures because of potential limits and embracing new methodologies that lack empirical validation. Further, transforming provocative results into facts increases the likelihood of generating more chaos in an area of inquiry in which it is already hard to know what is random and what has been replicated. On the basis of the evidence presented in this chapter, it seems premature, then, to conclude that the Strange Situation is invalid, that the Q-Sort methodology represents a significant improvement over it, or that the determinants and correlates of attachment security vary across ecological niches, namely, those in which infants are and are not exposed to extensive nonparental care.

References

Ainslie, R. C. "The Social Ecology of Day Care Children with Secure and Insecure Maternal Attachment." Paper presented at the annual meeting of the American Psychological Association, New York City, August 28, 1987.

Ainsworth, M.D.S., and Wittig, B. "Attachment and Exploratory Behavior of One-Year-Olds in a Strange Situation." In B. M. Foss (ed.), *Determinants of Infant Behavior*. Vol. 4. London: Methuen, 1969.

Andersson, B. "Effects of Public Day Care: A Longitudinal Study." *Child Development*, 1989, *60* (4), 857–866.

Barglow, P., Vaughn, B. E., and Molitor, N. "Effects of Maternal Absence Due to Employment on the Quality of Infant-Mother Attachment in a Low-Risk Sample." *Child Development*, 1987, *58* (4), 945–954.

Belsky, J. "Infant Day Care: A Cause for Concern?" *Zero to Three*, 1986, *6* (5), 1–7.

Belsky, J. "The 'Effects' of Infant Day Care Reconsidered." *Early Childhood Research Quarterly*, 1988, *3* (3), 235–272.

Belsky, J. "Infant-Parent Attachment and Day Care: In Defense of the Strange Situation." In J. Lande and S. Scarr (eds.), *The Future of Child Care in the United States*. Hillsdale, N.J.: Erlbaum, 1989.

Belsky, J. "Developmental Risks Associated with Infant Day Care: Attachment Insecurity, Aggression, and Noncompliance?" In S. Chehrazi (ed.), *Balancing Work and Parenting: Psychological and Developmental Implications of Day Care*. New York: American Psychiatric Press, in press.

Belsky, J., and Isabella, R. "Maternal, Infant, and Social-Contextual Determinants of Attachment Security." In J. Belsky and T. Nezworski (eds.), *Clinical Implications of Attachment*. Hillsdale, N.J.: Erlbaum, 1988.

Belsky, J., and Rovine, M. "Temperament and Attachment Security in the Strange Situation: An Empirical Rapprochement." *Child Development*, 1987, *58* (3), 787–795.

Belsky, J., and Rovine, M. "Nonmaternal Care in the First Year of Life and Security of Infant-Parent Attachment." *Child Development*, 1988, *59* (1), 157–167.

Belsky, J., Rovine, M., and Fish, M. "The Developing Family System." In M. Gunnar (ed.), *Minnesota Symposia of Child Psychology*. Vol. 22: *Systems and Development*. Hillsdale, N.J.: Erlbaum, 1989.

Benn, R. "Factors Promoting Secure Attachment Relationships Between Employed Mothers and Their Sons." *Child Development*, 1986, *57* (5), 1224–1231.

Clarke-Stewart, K. A. " 'The "Effects" of Infant Day Care Reconsidered' Reconsidered: Risks for Parents, Children, and Researchers." *Early Childhood Research Quarterly*, 1988, *3* (3), 293–318.

Clarke-Stewart, K. A. "Infant Day Care: Maligned or Malignant?" *American Psychologist*, 1989, *44* (2), 266–273.

Epstein, S. "The Stability of Behavior: 1. On Predicting Most of the People Much of the Time." *Journal of Personality and Social Psychology*, 1979, *37* (7), 1097–1126.

Haskins, R. "Public School Aggression Among Children with Varying Day Care Experience." *Child Development*, 1985, *56* (3), 689–703.

Howes, C. "Can the Age of Entry and the Quality of Infant Child Care Predict Behaviors in Kindergarten?" *Developmental Psychology*, 1990, *26* (2), 292–303.

Jacobson, J. L., and Wille, D. E. "Influence of Attachment and Separation Experience on Separation Distress at 18 Months." *Developmental Psychology*, 1984, *20* (3), 477–484.

Phillips, D., McCartney, K., Scarr, S., and Howes, C. "Selective Review of Infant Day Care Research: A Cause for Concern." *Zero to Three*, 1987, 7 (3), 18–21.

Rushton, J. P., Brainerd, C. J., and Pressley, M. "Behavioral Development and Construct Validity: The Principle of Aggregation." *Psychological Bulletin*, 1983, 94 (1), 18–38.

Thompson, R. "The Effects of Infant Day Care Through the Prism of Attachment Theory: A Critical Appraisal." *Early Childhood Research Quarterly*, 1988, 3 (3), 273–282.

Waters, E., and Deane, K. E. "Defining and Assessing Individual Differences in Attachment Relationships: Q-Methodology and the Organization of Behavior in Infant and Early Childhood." In I. Bretherton and E. Waters (eds.), *Growing Points in Attachment Theory and Research*. Monographs of the Society for Research in Child Development, vol. 50, nos. 1–2 (serial no. 209). Chicago: University of Chicago Press, 1985.

Weinraub, M., Jaeger, E., and Hoffman, L. "Predicting Infant Outcome in Families of Employed and Non-Employed Mothers." *Early Childhood Research Quarterly*, 1988, 3 (4), 361–378.

Jay Belsky is a professor of human development in the Department of Human Development and Family Studies at The Pennsylvania State University, University Park.

Michael Rovine is an assistant professor of human development in the same department.

In a state with minimal child care standards, early, extensive alternative care arrangements were associated with pervasive negative effects in third graders.

Child Care and the Family: Complex Contributors to Child Development

Deborah Lowe Vandell, Mary Ann Corasaniti

One of the more daunting tasks facing researchers, policymakers, and parents is understanding the effects of alternative child care arrangements on child development. The stakes are high for individuals and society. On the one hand is evidence that participation in model, early education programs can have long-term salutary effects on low-income children (Consortium for Longitudinal Studies, 1983; Haskins, 1989). On the other hand are disquieting reports that early, extensive nonmaternal care may place children "at risk" for subsequent social and emotional problems. In particular, there is some evidence that children who have extensive nonmaternal care during infancy are more likely than children without such experience to avoid contact with their mothers (Belsky, 1988; Clarke-Stewart, 1989). With these potentially conflicting costs and benefits, there has been considerable pressure on researchers to provide answers for this major social policy question: Is alternative child care associated with long-term positive or negative developmental outcomes?

A short, simple answer to this question is not likely to be forthcoming. Recent research (Goelman and Pence, 1987; Hock, DeMeis, and McBride, 1988; Howes and Olenick, 1986; Kontos, 1987; McCartney and Galanopoulos, 1988) suggests that child care is a complex phenomenon intertwined with family functioning and child characteristics. Consequently, we will probably never be able to draw global conclusions like "child care is bad for children" or the converse "child care is good for children." Instead, any conclusions about child care must be carefully qualified in terms of

NEW DIRECTIONS FOR CHILD DEVELOPMENT, no. 49, Fall 1990 © Jossey-Bass Inc., Publishers

(1) the characteristics of the child care environment, (2) the characteristics of the families selecting the care, and (3) the characteristics of the children using the particular child care arrangement.

Variations in Child Care Environments

There is wide variability in the quality of child care provided in this country both within communities (Howes, 1989) and across states (Morgan, 1987; Phillips, McCartney, and Scarr, 1987). As an example of this diversity, states have very different child care standards (Morgan, 1987). Minimum ratios of caregivers-to-infants in center-based care range from 1:4 to 1:7. For four-year-olds, adult-child ratios range from 1:10 to 1:20.

Educational requirements for caregivers also vary widely. While three states require substantial college-level training, twenty-six states have no preservice educational requirements for teachers in day-care centers. Nine states have neither preservice nor inservice educational requirements for center-based caregivers.

State regulation of family day-care (FDC) homes is even more variable. Eleven states allow five or more infants to be cared for by a single provider, whereas twenty-two states restrict FDC homes to two infants (although with varying numbers of older children). The number of children typically permitted in FDC homes is six, but one state (Mississippi) allows up to fifteen children with a single caregiver. Twenty-seven states have neither preservice nor inservice educational requirements for FDC providers, while one state (Wisconsin) has substantial educational requirements for these providers.

The current study was conducted in Texas, a state with minimal child care standards. Texas has no educational requirements for FDC providers, and center-based caregivers are only required to have fifteen hours of inservice training per year, with no preservice requirements. Up to twelve children (including four infants) may be cared for by a single FDC provider. In center-based care, ratios of 1:6 for infants and 1:18 for four-year-olds are sanctioned.

These state standards are important because there is evidence that caregiver training, adult-child ratios, and group size are related to children's experiences within the child care setting and to child development outcomes (Howes, 1989; Ruopp, Travers, Glantz, and Coelen, 1979; Vandell, Henderson, and Wilson, 1988). Children who attend programs with poorly trained teachers, large classes, and poor ratios spend less time interacting positively with teachers and more time in aimless wandering. Furthermore, when observed four years later, children who attended such programs were judged to be less socially competent and more unhappy than children who had attended higher-quality child care programs (Vandell, Henderson, and Wilson, 1988). It is clear that any conclusions about child care effects must be made in the context of the particular child care standards imposed by the state or community.

Conclusions about child care may also vary depending on the amount of care each week (Clarke-Stewart and Gruber, 1984; Vlietstra, 1981) and the age children begin care (Belsky, 1988). Some children attend nursery schools for a few hours a day, while other children have more extensive experiences in alternative child care. For some children alternative care starts during infancy, while others start at preschool or school age. Children in Scandinavian countries with national parental leave policies typically begin child care after infancy (Andersson, 1987; Lamb and others, 1988). Belsky's (1988) argument about heightened attachment insecurity pertains only to children who begin extensive alternative care as infants.

The study of child care is further complicated by a confounding of prior and ongoing child care arrangements. Howes (1989) observed that children who previously attended poor-quality programs were more likely to be currently attending poor-quality programs. Vandell, Henderson, and Wilson (1988) noted that differences in children's after-school care were associated with earlier child care arrangements. The question is, "If prior care and current care are confounded, to which do you attribute effects?" A more parsimonious explanation of differences in child functioning may be current child care experiences.

Confounding of Child Care and Family Factors

In addition to considering child care characteristics, the study of child care cannot be made in isolation of family situations. Families who select different child care programs often differ in terms of childrearing values (Kontos, 1987; Phillips, McCartney, and Scarr, 1987), family stress (Howes and Olenick, 1986), parental education (Goelman and Pence, 1987; Kontos, 1987), social class (Vandell, Henderson, and Wilson, 1988), and parental marital status (Goelman and Pence, 1987). Less stressed, better educated, higher social class, maritally intact families are more likely to place their children in higher-quality care. Choices related to type of care (sitter versus center) may also be confounded with parental attitudes (Hock, DeMeis, and McBride, 1988) and economic resources (Clarke-Stewart and Gruber, 1984).

This confounding of child care and family factors is problematic for researchers because we cannot tell in nonlongitudinal research which comes first. In some instances, families choosing a particular child care arrangement may differ a priori from families who make other child care choices. These self-selection differences may lead us to conclude erroneously that child care is a major contributor to child outcomes when, in fact, other preexisting family or child characteristics are responsible.

At the same time, there is another family and child care connection that has rarely been studied. Some differences between families may emerge over time as a result of the combination of child care and parenting situations. For example, family or, more specifically, marital relationships might be negatively affected by the parents' long work hours or problems in child care arrangements (Owen and Cox, 1988). If child care and maternal employment precipitate changes in the family, then it is not appropriate to think of these family differences as a priori self-selection factors.

Individual Differences in Reactions to Child Care

In addition to confounding of child care and family factors, it is possible that the same child care arrangement is experienced differently by different children. Thus, there are arguments that boys and girls may react differently to extensive child care, with boys being more vulnerable to negative effects of infant care (Belsky and Rovine, 1988; Chase-Lansdale, 1989; Gamble and Zigler, 1986). Parental marital status (Belsky and Rovine, 1988) is another possible moderator of child care effects. It could be that child care and divorce act as dual stressors that cumulatively exert a greater effect than either factor alone. Alternatively, child care could act as a buffer to minimize the effects of a family disruption. Family social class is a third possible moderator. Children from lower socioeconomic status (SES) families may benefit more from high-quality child care than do children from more affluent families, but they may also be more negatively affected by poor-quality care. To date, there has been very little work examining these possible interactive effects.

In the current study, child care effects were examined within the context of mediating and moderating influences. Two major questions were addressed: (1) Are there long-term effects associated with extent of care and age of entry into child care in a state with minimal child care regulations? (2) Are there differential child care effects associated with family marital status, child gender, or social class?

Methodology of the Current Study

Parents of 349 third graders were asked to recall for each year of their children's lives (zero to one, one to two, two to three, and so on) if they had used regular alternative care, if that care was more or less than thirty hours a week, and the form of care (day-care center, family day care, in-home sitter, nursery, or preschool).

Because this was a retrospective data set, we could not directly establish the accuracy of these parental recollections. Two other sources for estimating reliability of parental recall were used. The Timberlawn Young Family Project (Owen and Cox, 1988) interviewed mothers of twelve-month-olds about their employment and child care arrangements during the first year of their children's lives. When the children were four-and-one-half years old, mothers were given the child care questionnaire used in the current study. As a reliability assessment, agreement between maternal reports at twelve months and four-and-one-half years were compared. Agreement on whether they had used regular care was 100 percent (26 of 26 cases). Agreement about type of care was 82 percent (22 of 26 cases). Agreement about extent of care was 88 percent (23 of 26 cases).

A second test of parental recall used the longitudinal sample studied by Vandell, Henderson, and Wilson (1988). Children were first observed at four years of age, and child care information was collected at their child care centers. Four years later parents completed the questionnaire used in the current study. Recall of whether they used care, type of care, and extent of care was 100 percent. Given these responses, we feel confident that parents were able to accurately report retrospectively if they had used child care and roughly the extent of care (that is, more or less than thirty hours a week).

Based on the parental reports, 236 children (92 boys) were selected for this study. These were all of the white children in the sample who had participated in one of five child care histories: stayed home with mother until kindergarten (N = 37, 14 boys), began part-time care after the first year (N = 119, 46 boys), began part-time care during the first year and continued until public school (N = 18, 7 boys), stayed with the mother during the first year and began extensive care after the first year (N = 20, 6 boys), and began extensive child care during the first year (N = 42, 18 boys). Extensive care was defined as more than thirty hours a week in nonmaternal care.

Multiple assessments were made of the third graders' functioning, including (1) teachers' 5-point ratings of the children's peer relationships, work habits, compliance, and emotional health using a thirty-two-item questionnaire; (2) parent ratings of the children's peer relationships, work habits, emotional health, and compliance using the same 5-point scales; (3) positive and negative sociometric nominations based on classmates' naming of three same-sex classmates they "liked to play with" and three same-sex classmates they "did not play with"; (4) children's 4-point ratings of themselves socially, cognitively, physically, and generally, using the Harter Scale of Social Competence; (5) report card academic grades (reading, language, and math) averaged across the first, second, and third grades, with higher scores designating poorer grades; (6) report card conduct grades for work/study skills and interpersonal relations averaged across all three grades, with higher scores designating poorer marks; and (7) standardized test scores including the Comprehensive Test of Basic Skills (CTBS), the Cognitive Abilities Test (an IQ test), the Iowa Test of Basic Skills (ITBS), and the Texas Assessment of Basic Skills (TABS).

Contrasts of Five Child Care Histories

Using this data set, questions about the potential influences of child care history were addressed. The first question was simply whether there were differences in the children associated with child care history. For these analyses, five types of child care history (exclusive maternal care, part-time care beginning after infancy, part-time care beginning during infancy, extensive care beginning after infancy, and extensive care beginning during infancy) were contrasted using one-way multivariate analyses of variance (MANOVAs and ANOVAs), followed by Duncan post hoc analyses.

As shown in Table 1, differences in teacher ratings, parent ratings, peer nominations, self-assessments, report card grades, and standardized test scores were associated with child care history. Thus, child care differences were apparent in every set of variables studied. According to both teachers and parents, children who began extensive child care during infancy had poorer peer relationships, poorer emotional well-being, and poorer work habits and were harder to discipline than children who had been in part-time child care or exclusive maternal care. Children who began extensive child care as infants also received more negative peer nominations from their classmates. Their grades on academic report cards, as well as grades on work habits and interpersonal skills, also were poorer.

In some areas, children who began extensive care after infancy also performed poorly. Like children with extensive infant care, these children had poorer academic, interpersonal, and work habits grades than children in part-time or exclusive maternal care. Teachers reported that they had poorer work habits than children in part-time or exclusive maternal care. In addition, they rated themselves more negatively in social, cognitive, and general abilities than children with less extensive child care histories.

The next step was to determine if there were family differences that might be confounded with child care choices. As shown in Table 2, family factors and child care choices were often confounded. In contrast to children who had been in extensive child care or exclusive maternal care, children in part-time care came from more highly educated families. Their fathers had higher-status occupations. In contrast, children who had been in extensive child care moved more often. Their families were smaller and were more likely to be divorced. There were also differences in their current after-school arrangements: third graders who had been in more extensive child care were less likely to return home to their mothers after school.

Child Care History as a Predictor of Child Outcomes

The question, then, is which of these child care, family, and child characteristics best predict child outcomes for the third graders. To answer this

Table 1. Comparisons on Social and Cognitive Variables by Child Care History

Variables	Child Care History					F
	Exclusive Maternal Care	Part-Time After Infancy	Part-Time During Infancy	Extensive After Infancy	Extensive During Infancy	
Teacher ratings [MANOVA F (16, 878)]						4.04[e]
Peer relations	4.3[a]	4.2[a]	4.2[a]	4.0[a]	3.6[b]	8.63[e]
Work habits	4.0[a]	3.6	3.7[a]	3.1[b]	3.0[b]	5.20[e]
Emotional health	3.7	3.8[a]	3.8[a]	3.6	3.3[b]	3.27[d]
Compliance	4.5[a]	4.2[a]	4.4[a]	4.1[a]	3.4[b]	6.69[e]
Parent ratings [MANOVA F (16, 878)]						4.47[e]
Peer relations	4.2[a]	4.2[a]	4.1[a]	4.1[a]	3.9[b]	5.22[e]
Work habits	3.9[a]	3.8[a]	3.8[a]	3.4	3.2[b]	6.14[e]
Emotional health	4.1[a]	4.2[a]	4.1[a]	4.2[a]	3.8[b]	
Compliance	4.4[a]	4.1[a]	4.1[a]	4.1[a]	3.1[b]	11.00[e]
Peer nominations [MANOVA F (8, 428)]						2.12[c]
Positive	3.2	3.4	3.1	2.6	2.3	2.06[c]
Negative	1.7[a]	2.0[a]	1.9[a]	2.9	3.6[b]	6.01[e]
Self ratings [MANOVA F (16, 818)]						2.34[d]
General	3.2[a]	3.1	3.4[a]	2.8[b]	3.0	2.16
Social	2.8[a]	3.0[a]	3.0[a]	2.4[b]	2.8[a]	2.88[c]
Cognitive	3.2[a]	3.2[a]	3.2[a]	2.7[b]	3.0	4.08[d]
Physical	2.9	3.1	3.2[a]	2.7[b]	2.9	
Report card grades [MANOVA F (12, 662)]						2.52[d]
Grade point average	3.2[a]	3.2[a]	3.2[a]	3.9[b]	4.2[b]	6.01[e]
Work habits	1.6[a]	1.6[a]	1.6[a]	2.0[b]	1.9[b]	7.22[e]
Interpersonal	1.5[a]	1.5[a]	1.4[a]	1.7[b]	1.7[b]	4.34[e]
Standardized test scores [MANOVA F (16, 598)]						1.87[c]
IQ	116.5	114.3	113.6	110.1	109.8	
CTBS	64.1	68.6[a]	63.6	48.1[b]	54.3	3.07[c]
ITBS	75.3	76.3	75.3	64.8	64.7	3.60[d]
TABS	28.5	29.2	29.5	28.7	29.1	

Note: Parent and teacher ratings were on 5-point scales. Higher scores designate more positive ratings. Sociometric nominations were prorated to correct for class size. All were adjusted as if there were twelve same-sex children in the class. Academic and conduct grades were scored such that better grades were designated by lower numbers. Scores for the Iowa Test of Basic Skills (ITBS) and the Comprehensive Test of Basic Skills (CTBS) were based on national percentiles. Scores on the Texas Assessment of Basic Skills (TABS) were absolute scores. Empty F cells indicate nonsignificant F values.

[a, b] Scores are significantly different as determined by Duncan post hoc analyses.
[c] $p < .05$
[d] $p < .01$
[e] $p < .001$

Table 2. Family and Child Characteristics Associated with Differences in Child Care History

Characteristics	Exclusive Maternal Care	Part-Time After Infancy	Part-Time During Infancy	Extensive After Infancy	Extensive During Infancy	Significance Value
	Child Care History					
	Means					F
Father education	3.7[b]	4.6[a]	5.1[a]	3.4[b]	3.6[b]	8.29[e]
Mother education	2.7[b]	3.9[a]	4.1[a]	2.8[b]	3.0[b]	11.13[e]
Father occupation	50.5[b]	58.4[a]	61.4[a]	47.4[b]	51.1[b]	6.39[e]
SES (composite)	−.69[b]	.41[a]	.74[a]	−.82[b]	−.46[b]	11.44[e]
Family moves	1.1	.5[a]	.6[a]	1.5[b]	1.5[b]	7.97[e]
Number of children	2.7[a]	2.4	2.4	2.1[b]	2.0[b]	3.12[c]
Child birth order	2.0	1.9	1.9	1.8	1.5	
	Frequencies					χ^2
After school						
Mother	21	86	11	3	3	92.80[e]
Latchkey	6	9	3	7	17	
Center/sitter	2	4	1	7	17	
Marital status						
Married	24	94	14	10	19	41.79[e]
Divorced/separated	5	5	1	7	18	

Note: Mean differences were tested using 5-way ANOVAs. Frequency differences were tested using χ^2.

[a, b] Scores are significantly different as determined by Duncan post hoc analyses.
[c] $p < .05$
[d] $p < .01$
[e] $p < .001$

question, stepwise regressions were used. Stepwise regression (Pedhauser, 1982) has been viewed as an appropriate strategy for exploratory research in which one does not know which array of variables will be the "best" predictors of outcomes. Stepwise regressions do not assume a priori that one variable assumes precedence over another. Instead, they tell us (1) which single variable of a larger array of variables accounts for the largest proportion of the variance, and (2) which combination of variables predicts the largest proportion of the variance.

In the current study, six child and family variables were included in the stepwise regressions: (1) family SES, the principal component composite score of maternal and paternal occupation status, (2) family size, (3) family marital status, (4) number of family moves, (5) child birth order, and (6) child gender. The regressions also include child care history coded as a continuous variable with 1 equaling exclusive maternal care, 2 equaling part-time care beginning after infancy, 3 equaling part-time care beginning during infancy, 4 equaling extensive care beginning after infancy, and 5 equaling extensive care beginning during infancy. Current after-school care was dummy coded for mother care, latchkey, and other adult-supervised care. Finally, three interaction terms (child care history × marital status, history × social class, and history × child gender) were included within the stepwise regressions.

These particular child and family variables were selected for inclusion because of their documented importance to child development. We hoped to ascertain the relative importance of these other variables in comparison to child care history. The interaction terms were included because of recent speculation about the importance of mediating factors.

Prior to conducting the stepwise regressions, zero-order correlations between the predictor variables were computed. As shown in Table 3, some minimal to moderate relations between variables were obtained. These relations were not large enough to argue that collinearity was a major problem. Consequently, the stepwise regressions were completed.

As shown in Table 4, child care history was the single best predictor of teacher and parental ratings of peer relationships, compliance, work habits, and emotional health, with children who had participated in more extensive care receiving more negative ratings. Child care history was also the single best predictor of the classmates' positive and negative nominations. Children with more extensive child care experience received fewer positive nominations and more negative nominations from peers. Children's academic and conduct grades were also best predicted by child care history, with extensive infant care being associated with poorer grades. Finally, children's CTBS scores were negatively predicted by extensive child care experience.

Table 3. Zero-Order Correlations Between Predictor Variables

	Mother After School	Latchkey	SES	Marital Status	Family Moves	Family Size	Child Birth Order	Child Gender
Child care history	$-.57^b$	$.32^b$	$-.15^a$	$-.31^b$	$.22^b$	$-.25^b$	$-.16^a$	.00
Mother after-school care		$-.68^c$	$.22^a$	$.46^b$	$-.24^b$	$.16^a$	$-.08$	.00
Latchkey			$-.24^b$	$-.28^b$	$.22^b$	.04	$.23^b$	.01
Family SES				$.19^b$	$-.19^b$	$-.07$	.00	.09
Marital status					$-.42^b$	$.13^a$	.09	.08
Family moves						$-.05$	.09	$-.06$
Family size							$-.05$	$-.03$
Child birth order								.09

Note: SES = socioeconomic status

[a] $p < .05$
[b] $p < .01$
[c] $p < .001$

Table 4. Single Best Predictor of Child Outcomes Derived from Step 1 of Stepwise Regressions

Outcomes	Best Predictor	Beta	R^2
Teacher ratings			
Peer relations	Child care history	-.35	.12[c]
Compliance	Child care history	-.31	.10[c]
Work habits	Child care history	-.31	.09[c]
Emotional health	Child care history	-.22	.05[c]
Parent ratings			
Peer relations	Child care history	-.27	.07[c]
Compliance	Child care history	-.39	.15[c]
Work habits	Child care history	-.31	.09[c]
Emotional health	After school care	.23	.05[c]
Peer nominations			
Positive	Child care history	-.17	.02[a]
Negative	Child care history	.30	.08[c]
Self-assessments			
Cognitive	Family marital status	.28	.07[b]
Social	Family marital status	.20	.04[b]
General	Family marital status	.22	.04[b]
Physical	Child sex	.28	.07[c]
Report card grades			
Grade point average	Child care history	.32	.10[c]
Work habits	Child care history	.34	.10[c]
Interpersonal	Child care history	.27	.07[c]
Standardized tests			
IQ	SES composite	.24	.06[c]
CTBS	Child care history	-.20	.04[b]
ITBS	SES by history interaction	.29	.08[c]
TABS	Child birth order	-.14	.02[a]

Note: SES = socioeconomic status, CTBS = Comprehensive Test of Basic Skills, ITBS = Iowa Test of Basic Skills, TABS = Texas Assessment of Basic Skills.
[a] $p < .05$
[b] $p < .01$
[c] $p < .001$

Only one variable was best predicted by the children's current after-school care arrangement. Parents rated children who returned home to their mothers after school more positively in terms of their emotional well-being.

For other variables, family characteristics were better predictors of child outcomes. Children's self-assessments of their social, cognitive, and general competencies and their interpersonal report card grades were best predicted by family marital status. IQ was best predicted by the SES composite. Birth order was the best predictor of TABS scores.

The final question concerned what combination of child care and family variables provided the best model of the third graders' performances.

Here, only variables making unique contributions to the model at the $p < .05$ level were retained. As shown in Table 5, for most variables, child outcomes were best predicted by a combination of child care history and family factors. Child care history was a significant contributor to teacher and parent ratings of peer relations, work habits, and compliance, and to teacher ratings of emotional health, with more extensive care associated with more negative assessments. Extensive child care also predicted fewer positive and more negative nominations from classmates, lower cognitive self-assessments, poorer academic and work habits grades, and lower IQ, CTBS, and ITBS scores.

In addition, child and family factors were significant contributors to child outcomes. For example, the social class composite significantly contributed to teacher ratings of peer relationships, to grades on academic work, work habits, and interpersonal conduct, and to IQ and ITBS scores. Parental marital status significantly predicted children's self-assessments, grades on academic work, work habits, and interpersonal skills, negative peer nominations, and teacher ratings of compliance. Children's birth order contributed to standardized test scores and to cognitive self-assessments.

Table 5. "Best" Model to Predict Child Outcomes Using Stepwise Regressions

Outcomes	Predictors			Adjusted R^2
	Child Care	Family/Child	Family and Child Care Interactions	
Teacher ratings				
Peer relations	History (-.31[c])	SES (.22[c]) Child sex (-.24[c])		.22[c]
Compliance	History (-.20[c])	Marital status (.17[b]) Child sex (-.21[b])	SES × history (.15[a])	.16[c]
Work habits	History (-.32[c])	Birth order (-.20[b]) Child sex (-.17[b])		.15[c]
Emotional health	History (-.22[b])			.05[b]
Parent Ratings				
Peer relations	History (-.24[c])	Marital status (.18[b]) Child sex (-.21[a]) Family size (-.14[a])		.14[c]
Compliance	History (-.30[c])	Marital status (.20) Birth order (.14)		.20[c]
Work habits	History (-.36[c])	Child sex (-.19[b])	Marriage × history (.14[a])	.13[c]
Emotional health	Mother after school (.23[c])			.05[c]
Sociometric nominations				
Positive	History (-.17[a])			.03[a]

Table 5. *(continued)*

Outcomes	Predictors			Adjusted R^2
	Child Care	Family/Child	Family and Child Care Interactions	
Sociometric nominations *(continued)*				
Negative	History (.21[b])	Marital status (-.14[a])	SES × history (-.16[b])	.12[c]
Self-assessments				
Cognitive	History (-.21[b])	Marital status (.22[b]) Birth order (-.16[a])		.12[c]
Social		Marital status (.20[b])		.04[b]
General		Marital status (.22[b])		.04[b]
Physical		Child sex (.28[c])		.07[c]
Report card grades				
Grade point average	History (.30[c]) Latchkey (-.13[a])	SES (-.24[c]) Family size (.14[a]) Marital status (-.13[a]) Child sex (.12[a])		.18[c]
Work habits	History (.23[c])	SES (-.21[b]) Marital status (-.21[b]) Child sex (.28[c]) Birth order (.14[a])		.25[c]
Interpersonal	Mother afterschool (-.32[b]) Latchkey (-.31[b])	SES (-.21[b]) Marital status (-.24[b]) Birth order (.13[a])	Sex × history (.23[c])	.20[c]
Standardized tests				
IQ	History (-.29[b])	SES (.21[b]) Birth order (-.23[b]) Family moves (.15[a])	Marriage × history (.15[a])	.17[c]
CTBS	History (-.37[c]) Latchkey (.19[a])	Birth order (-.21[b]) SES (.48[b])	Sex × history (.17[a]) Sex × history (-.34[b])	.18[c]
ITBS	History (-.24[b])	Birth order (-.24[b])		.18[c]
TABS		Birth order (-.14[a])		.02[a]

Note: These variables were selected via stepwise regressions as forming the "best" predictors of child outcomes. Variables were retained for the model only if they made a significant ($p < .05$) contribution. The numbers in parentheses are the betas for each variable. SES = socioeconomic status, CTBS = Comprehensive Test of Basic Skills, ITBS = Iowa Test of Basic Skills, TABS = Texas Test of Basic Skills.

[a] $p < .05$
[b] $p < .01$
[c] $p < .001$

A third set of contributors to child outcomes was also apparent. As is evident in the third column of Table 5, effects of child care history were sometimes moderated by family and child characteristics. These interactions were consistent with a "risk" approach to child care history, with extensive infant care being associated with more negative developmental outcomes. For example, IQ scores were lowest for children whose parents were divorced *and* who began extensive child care during infancy. These same children received the poorest work habits ratings from parents.

Other interactive effects related to social class and child gender were found. Children were rated by their teachers as most difficult to discipline if they were from lower SES families and had been in extensive child care as infants. This subset of low-income children also received the most negative peer nominations. The interpersonal conduct grades were poorest for boys who had been in extensive child care since infancy, while girls who had been in extensive child care in infancy had the poorest CTBS scores.

Within these interactive effects, a second child care history, exclusive maternal care until kindergarten, was also associated with problematical development. As was the case with extensive infant care, IQ scores were lower for children from divorced families if they had been in exclusive maternal care. Exclusive maternal care was also associated with parental reports of greater difficulty in disciplining middle-class children. Boys who had been in exclusive maternal care had lower CTBS scores than if they had been in part-time care. There was no evidence of problematical functioning for children who were in part-time care, regardless of parental marital status, social class, or child gender.

Summary

In a state with minimal child care standards, we found pervasive differences in third graders associated with earlier child care histories. More extensive child care predicted children receiving more negative ratings from parents and teachers, poorer academic and conduct grades, lower standardized test scores, and more negative sociometric nominations. In addition, for some variables (IQ, work habits, negative peer nominations, and compliance ratings) there was evidence of interactive effects in which both extensive infant care and exclusive maternal care were associated with more problematical functioning, depending on parental marital status, social class, and child gender. We found no evidence of negative effects associated with part-time care.

This study has several important limitations that should be acknowledged. The first is the danger of generalizing these results to states and communities with higher-quality child care standards than those imposed in Texas. They may, unfortunately, be generalizable to the twenty states with child care regulations similar to those in Texas.

This study has another important limitation. It did not examine the underlying processes that might contribute to the effects of child care history. For example, we do not know if the differences in children who were in part-time versus extensive child care are owing to (1) differences in the children's experiences while they are in the child care settings, or (2) differences in the quality of interactions that occur when the two groups of children are at home, or (3) some combination of children's experiences in child care and the family.

References

Andersson, B. E. "The Importance of Public Day-Care for Preschool Children's Later Development." Paper presented at the biennial meeting of the Society for Research in Child Development, Baltimore, Maryland, April 1987.

Belsky, J. "The 'Effects' of Infant Day Care Reconsidered." *Early Childhood Research Quarterly,* 1988, 3 (3), 235–272.

Belsky, J., and Rovine, M. J. "Nonmaternal Care in the First Year of Life and Security of Infant-Parent Attachment." *Child Development,* 1988, 59 (1), 157–167.

Chase-Lansdale, L. "Maternal Employment During Infancy: Insights from 'Children of the NLSY.' " Paper presented at the biennial meeting of the Society for Research in Child Development, Kansas City, Missouri, April 1989.

Clarke-Stewart, K. A. "Infant Day Care: Maligned or Malignant?" *American Psychologist,* 1989, 44 (2), 266–273.

Clarke-Stewart, K. A., and Gruber, C. P. "Day Care Forms and Features." In R. C. Ainslie (ed.), *The Child and the Day Care Setting: Qualitative Variations and Development.* New York: Praeger, 1984.

Consortium for Longitudinal Studies. *As the Twig Is Bent: Lasting Effects of Preschool Programs.* Hillsdale, N.J.: Erlbaum, 1983.

Gamble, T. J., and Zigler, E. "Effects of Infant Day Care: Another Look at the Evidence." *American Journal of Orthopsychiatry,* 1986, 56 (1), 26–42.

Goelman, H., and Pence, A. "Effects of Child Care, Family, and Individual Characteristics on Children's Language Development: The Victoria Day Care Research Project." In D. Phillips (ed.), *Quality in Child Care: What Does Research Tell Us?* Research Monograph of the National Association for the Education of Young Children, Vol. 1. Washington, D.C.: National Association for the Education of Young Children, 1987.

Haskins, R. "Beyond Metaphor: The Efficacy of Early Childhood Education." *American Psychologist,* 1989, 44 (2), 274–282.

Hock, E., DeMeis, D., and McBride, S. "Maternal Anxiety: Its Role in the Balance of Employment and Motherhood in Mothers of Infants." In A. E. Gottfried and A. W. Gottfried (eds.), *Maternal Employment and Children's Development: Longitudinal Research.* New York: Plenum, 1988.

Howes, C. "The Contribution of Caregiver Characteristics, Turnover, and Caregiving Competence to Child Development." Paper presented at the biennial meeting of the Society for Research in Child Development, Kansas City, Missouri, April 1989.

Howes, C., and Olenick, M. "Family and Child Care Influences on Toddlers' Compliance." *Child Development,* 1986, 57 (1), 202–216.

Kontos, S. "Day Care Quality, Family Background, and Children's Development." Paper presented at the biennial meeting of the Society for Research in Child Development, Baltimore, Maryland, April 1987.

Lamb, M. E., Hwang, C., Bookstein, F. L., Broberg, A., Hult, G., and Frodi, M. "Determinants of Social Competence in Swedish Preschoolers." *Developmental Psychology*, 1988, 24 (1), 58–70.

McCartney, K., and Galanopoulos, A. "Child Care and Attachment: A New Frontier the Second Time Around." *American Journal of Orthopsychiatry*, 1988, 58 (1), 16–24.

Morgan, G. *The National State of Child Care Regulation: 1986.* Watertown, Mass.: Work/Family Directions, 1987.

Owen, M. T., and Cox, M. J. "Maternal Employment and the Transition to Parenthood." In A. E. Gottfried and A. W. Gottfried (eds.), *Maternal Employment and Children's Development: Longitudinal Research.* New York: Plenum, 1988.

Pedhauser, E. J. *Multiple Regression in Behavioral Research.* (2nd ed.) New York: Holt, Rinehart & Winston, 1982.

Phillips, D., McCartney, K., and Scarr, S. "Child Care Quality and Children's Social Development." *Developmental Psychology*, 1987, 23 (4), 537–543.

Ruopp, R., Travers, J., Glantz, F., and Coelen, C. *Children at the Center: Final Results of the National Day Care Study.* Boston: Abt Associates, 1979.

Vandell, D. L., Henderson, V. K., and Wilson, K. S. "A Longitudinal Study of Children with Day-Care Experiences of Varying Quality." *Child Development*, 1988, 59 (5), 1286–1292.

Vlietstra, A. "Full- Versus Half-Day Preschool Attendance: Effects in Young Children as Assessed by Teacher Ratings and Behavioral Observations." *Child Development*, 1981, 52 (2), 603–610.

Deborah Lowe Vandell is a professor of educational psychology at the University of Wisconsin, Madison.

Mary Ann Corasaniti is a graduate student at the University of Texas, Dallas.

The results of two studies suggest that in child care of reasonably
good quality, home variables may be more important than
center variables in moderating security of attachment.

Family and Center Contributions to the Adjustment of Infants in Full-Time Day Care

Ricardo C. Ainslie

Most researchers agree that there is little empirical evidence to suggest that enrollment in day care after the first year of life poses a risk factor for the socioemotional development of the child. There are differences of opinion on the question of whether enrollment in day care during the first year, especially on a full-time basis, poses a risk factor; even among researchers who have reported heightened levels of insecure attachment for day-care children, there is consensus that not all children enrolled in day care are at risk. Thus, the pressing need is to identify the conditions of risk for those children who enter day care early.

Security of attachment has long been regarded as a function of the quality of the relationship between the infant and the individuals primarily responsible for the infant's care. Hence, studies of infant-caregiver and of infant-mother interaction involving children in nonmaternal care provide an important basis for understanding how specific factors may moderate risk. In one of the most extensive studies of infant-caregiver interaction in the day-care center, Jacobson and Owen (1987) found that caregivers were quite narrow in their interactions with the infants in their care. Particularly worrisome was their finding that caregiver level of stimulation was low and lacked variety, with infrequent play with words and toys, and infrequent interactions characterized by high levels of affect. These authors expressed

I thank Jay Belsky, Kathleen McCartney, and Brian Vaughn for their comments on this chapter.

some concern regarding what they felt was a lack of attention given to the total development of the child.

In another study, McCartney, Scarr, Phillips, Grajek, and Schwarz (1982) found that poor emotional adjustment, as rated by the caregivers, was related both to the age at entry into group care and to the quality of the day-care environments. The total maladjustment scores for these children were predicted by early entry into group care at centers that were rated high in overall quality and in verbal interaction. Thus, this study suggested that center-based variables play an important role in moderating potentially negative day-care effects.

A comparison between the quality of interaction that a child receives when with mother and when with caregiver is clearly pertinent to understanding the child's day-care experience. Stith and Davis (1984) compared mothers and caregivers (in family day-care settings) on social dimensions of the caregiving environment. They found few differences between employed and nonemployed mothers in their caregiving behaviors. However, Stith and Davis found a number of important differences when they compared the quality of interactions between the two groups of mothers and the children's caregivers. The nonemployed mothers exceeded the caregivers in the frequency of their contingent vocalizations, social play, expression of positive affect, and encouragement of emerging gross-motor responses and in the overall level and variety of social stimulation provided to the infants. These researchers also found that a more varied array of objects and toys was provided to the infants at home than in the day-care settings. Similar but even more extensive differences were obtained between the employed mothers and caregivers in interaction with the same infants. In addition to differences in contingent vocalizations, social play, socially mediated stimulation, and both level and variety of social stimulation, the employed mothers also exceeded their children's caregivers in the total frequency of tactile-kinesthetic, visual, and auditory stimulation provided to their infants. These results led Stith and Davis to conclude that their infant subjects "experienced less stimulating and responsive care and environments in the homes of their sitters than they did in their own homes regardless of whether their mothers were employed or not" (1984, p. 1345).

Not only did the employed mothers in the Stith and Davis study engage their infants in more intensive, varied, and responsive reciprocal interactions than the substitute caregivers, they also exceeded them in the sheer quantity of infant-directed touches, looks, and vocalizations, whether reciprocated or not by the infants. They concluded that most likely the long periods of daily separation were responsible for the enhanced frequency of mother-initiated, physical-sensory contacts with the infants.

In comparing three groups of children, two in day care (high quality and low quality) and one in exclusive maternal care, Peterson and Peterson (1986) found that verbal interaction between mother and child was more sustained and interactive in the home-care children, especially when compared with the children in poor-quality day care. The latter children were reported to engage seldomly in dyadic verbal interchange, even when their mothers were fully attentive to them. Peterson and Peterson speculated that this difference was due to variations in the children's experience, with home-care children spending more time verbally interacting with their mothers. However, they also found the same differences between the two day-care groups, who presumably experienced the same amount of time with their mothers. Similarly, Howes and Rubenstein (1985) concluded that only those toddlers cared for in relatively small groups and with favorable adult-to-child ratios have experiences comparable to those of toddlers at home. Finally, unlike Stith and Davis, who found employed mothers to be higher on some interactive behaviors than nonemployed mothers, Zaslow, Pedersen, Suwalsky, Cain, and Fivel (1985) reported that parents in dual wage-earner families provided their babies with less tactile stimulation, perhaps because of "the overload experienced" by these couples.

Such studies suggest that if there are consistent differences between day-care and non-day-care children, these may not necessarily be due to day care per se. Rather, different family or parental variables may well play at least as important a role as the day-care experience, when quality of day care is controlled (Phillips, McCartney, Scarr, and Howes, 1987). For example, Everson, Sarnat, and Ambron (1984) found a strong relationship between maternal attitudes toward day care and the extent of cooperation, compliance, persistence, and prosocial behavior in their day-care children. In that study, day-care children whose mothers had initially expressed no reluctance in placing them in day care were rated less positively on these dimensions than day-care children whose mothers had expressed greater reluctance to place them in out-of-home care. Similarly, other researchers have found links between working mothers' desire for motherhood (Farber and Egeland, 1982) or their marital satisfaction (Benn, 1986; Belsky and Rovine, 1988) and security of attachment in their children. These studies suggest that home-based variables moderate security of attachment in day-care children.

Many different forces contribute to the development of the day-care child. The literature summarized above indicates that both center- and home-based variables may play an important role in moderating the quality of experience of children enrolled in full-time day care beginning in infancy and hence their potential risk for developing insecure attachments. In this chapter, two studies are presented that examine moderators of adjustment in children who have been in full-time day care since infancy. In the first, center variables, including infant-caregiver interactions, are examined in relation to security of attachment. In the second study, home-based variables, including parental stress, satisfaction in parenting, and the family environment, are examined in relation to security of attachment.

Finally, in both studies the quality of the links between the home and the day-care environments, reflected in the degree of parental contact or involvement with their child's center, were studied in relation to security of attachment.

Study 1: Center-Based Variables and Attachment

Subjects. Thirty-four infants, their mothers, and their respective caregivers were recruited from ten community-based day-care centers judged to be of moderate-to-good quality. All centers were comparable in terms of caregiver-child ratio (2:12), number of children enrolled, curriculum, daily routines, and presence of age-appropriate toys and facilities. All centers were licensed to operate infant and preschool programs. University-based and pilot programs were excluded from the study, as were day-care centers judged to be of poor quality based on poor infant-caregiver ratios or inadequate facilities and materials. The majority of the centers included in this study were church sponsored, and all had programs for children from birth through the preschool years.

Subjects ranged from ten to eighteen months of age ($M = 13.4$). All were from intact, middle-class, Caucasian families in which both parents were working full-time. All children had been in full-time day care ($M = 41.5$ hours per week) for at least four months and with their respective caregivers for at least three months at the time of observation.

Fifteen caregivers also participated in the study. These women ranged in age from twenty-one to sixty-four years ($M = 40.3$). Their educational levels ranged from eighth grade to two years of graduate school work ($M = 12.4$).

Procedure. When the infants were between twelve and fifteen months old, attachment to their mothers and caregivers was assessed with the standard Strange Situation procedure (Ainsworth, Blehar, Waters, and Wall, 1978). The two sessions were scheduled three months apart, with mother-infant and caregiver-infant observations counterbalanced to prevent potential order effects. Videotaped observations were subsequently coded by Alan Sroufe and his colleagues at the University of Minnesota according to the standard classification scheme specified by Ainsworth, Blehar, Waters, and Wall (1978). Interobserver agreement for major classifications on these videotapes was 92 percent. Coders were blind to the purposes of the study. However, in approximately 50 percent of the caregiver-infant strange situations racial differences between infants and their caregivers may have indicated to the coders that the women involved in the Strange Situation Assessment were not the infants' mothers. Caregivers completed the Infant Characteristics Scales. This measure was developed for this study and consists of twenty-five Likert-type items (each with a range of 1–5). The self-administered questionnaire rated mothers' and caregivers' perceptions of the infants on the following seven dimensions: Affiliation, Activity Level,

Emotionality, Affect Quality, Exploration, Physicality, and Adaptiveness. Internal consistency for these dimensions ranged from .55 to .75.

On at least two separate occasions, each infant was observed in the day-care setting for a total of two hours of observations per child. Observations were made during regular free-play periods in the infant room when the majority of the infants were awake and not eating. Infants' behaviors were coded only for the primary caregiver and not for the room aide. Caregivers were told that observers were interested in the infants' behaviors in their presence. A contact was defined as any dyadic verbal, nonverbal, or physical interaction between infant and caregiver. Frequencies of seven categories of infant behavior were collected: independent activity, total contact, distress, misbehavior, contact seeking, duration of contact, and physical contact. Two observers were present for these observations. Differences in their observations were resolved afterward, and a consensus protocol was generated. On a random selection of 20 percent of the protocols, reliabilities (prior to consensus) ranged from 73 percent agreement to 83 percent agreement on sampled events. The observers were blind to other assessment data.

A semi-structured interview was also conducted with each of the mothers. This interview included demographic information as well as questions related to mothers' perceptions of their infants' day care, and mothers' and fathers' involvement in daily aspects of the day-care situation (for example, who brings the child to day care and extent of contact with the caregiver).

Results. A series of preliminary analyses revealed no sex differences on measures of interest and no order effects for the Strange Situation. The distribution of mother-infant attachment classifications was as follows: 61.8 percent (N = 21) of the children were classified as securely attached (B), 8.8 percent (N = 3) as insecure-avoidant (A), and 29.4 percent (N = 10) as insecure-resistant (C). The distribution of infant-caregiver classifications was as follows: 52 percent (N = 18) securely attached, 26.4 percent (N = 9) insecure-avoidant, and 20.5 percent (N = 7) insecure-resistant. There was considerable overlap between infant-mother and infant-caregiver attachment classifications. In all but seven of the cases, infants were either securely attached (B) (48 percent) or insecurely attached (A + C) (28 percent) to both mother and caregiver. Three infants (10 percent) were securely attached to the caregiver but not to their mothers, while the remaining four infants (14 percent) were securely attached to their mothers but not to the caregiver.

A series of stepwise analyses of discriminant functions were conducted to predict general aspects of infant-caregiver contacts from attachment classifications (mother and caregiver, respectively). Neither discriminant function was significant, which suggests that the observation data did not predict the infant-mother or infant-caregiver Strange Situation classifications (see Table 1 for the descriptive statistics (frequencies) of infant behavior in interaction with the caregiver).

Table 1. Descriptive Statistics for Infant Behavior
in Interaction with Caregiver

	Independent Activity	Total Contact	Distress	Misbehavior	Contact Seeking	Duration of Contact	Physical Contact
M	17.0	32.1	3.8	4.0	8.4	38.2	16.9
SD	11.8	16.0	2.6	3.6	6.7	24.3	9.3
Range	1–56	5–71	0–9	0–13	0–29	6–115	2–37

Caregiver and maternal perceptions of infants, as measured on the Infant Characteristics Scale, were related to attachment classifications. For caregiver ratings and infant-caregiver attachment classifications, six of the seven scales were significant predictors in the discriminant-function equation (Affiliation, Activity Level, Emotionality, Affect Quality, Exploration, and Physicality) [Wilkes λ = .397, χ_2 (12) = 23.5, $p < .02$]. Using this equation, 67.7 percent of the infant-caregiver classifications could be correctly classified as A, B, or C (Table 2). In general, caregivers tended to give the most positive ratings to the infants classified as insecure-avoidant, with securely attached children receiving intermediate ratings and insecure-resistant children receiving the lowest ratings.

With respect to maternal perceptions and infant-mother attachment, only three of the seven scales were significant predictors (Activity Level, Adaptiveness, and Emotionality) [Wilkes λ = .586, χ_2 (6) = 14.4, $p < .02$]. Using the discriminant-function equation, 54.8 percent of the infant-mother classifications could be correctly classified. Mothers rated children classified as securely attached most positively, with insecure-resistant children receiving intermediate ratings and insecure-avoidant children receiving the lowest ratings.

The association between parental contact with centers and attachment classifications was examined with chi-square analyses. High mother contact was defined as regular contact with the center that was more than five minutes in duration on each occasion (by self-report) (N = 11, 32 percent);

Table 2. Descriptive Statistics for Substitute Caregiver Perceptions
of Infants' Characteristics and Infant-Caregiver Attachment Classifications

Group Membership (N)		Affiliation	Activity Level	Emotionality	Affect Quality	Exploration	Adaptiveness	Physicality
A (9)	M	6.44	12.77	11.00	5.66	7.00	7.00	5.44
	SD	2.78	3.89	5.09	1.72	2.78	3.27	2.35
B (15)	M	6.73	15.46	12.33	7.26	8.26	7.93	6.93
	SD	2.28	5.01	3.24	2.25	3.86	3.32	2.68
C (7)	M	7.00	14.28	13.42	8.00	8.85	8.42	5.42
	SD	2.70	4.30	4.11	2.00	2.79	3.50	2.76

the remainder of mothers were defined as low contact. High father contact was defined as any regular contact with the day-care center (N = 16, 47 percent).

A series of chi-square analyses indicated that parental contact with the center was strongly associated with quality of maternal attachment and caregiver attachment. Infants whose mothers were rated as high contact (N = 11, 32 percent) were significantly more likely to be classified as securely attached to their mothers [χ_2 (1, N = 34) = 5.84, p < .02] and to their caregivers [χ_2 (1, N = 34) = 3.73, p < .05]. Children with fathers rated as high contact (N = 16, 47 percent) were also significantly more likely to have secure attachments to their mothers [χ_2 (1, N = 34) = 4.86, p < .05], although no association was found with infant-caregiver attachment classifications. Infants whose parents were both rated high contact (N = 8, 24 percent) were also significantly more likely to have secure attachments to their mothers [χ_2 (1, N = 34) = 6.42, p < .02] and to their caregivers [χ_2 (1, N = 34) = 7.37, p < .01]. In fact, all children whose mothers and fathers were both rated as high contact had secure attachments to their mothers and to caregivers.

To summarize, in this first study center-based observations of infant-caregiver interactions appeared to have no relation to infant-caregiver or infant-mother attachment classifications. Mothers' and caregivers' perceptions of infants were related to security of attachment, although mothers tended to rate the securely attached infants most positively, whereas the caregivers tended to rate the insecure-avoidant infants most positively. Finally, securely attached infants tended to have mothers and fathers who were rated (separately and jointly) as having high contact with their child's day-care center.

Study 2: Home-Based Variables and Attachment

Subjects. The subjects in this study were forty-one mother-child dyads. They were recruited from eight church-based day-care centers judged to be of moderate-to-good quality. Six of the eight centers were the same as those that participated in the first study. All centers were comparable in terms of caregiver-child ratio (2:12), number of children enrolled, curriculum, daily routines, and presence of age-appropriate toys and facilities.

Subjects were from intact, middle-class, Caucasian families in which both parents were employed full-time. The children in this second study ranged in age from fifteen to twenty-seven months (M = 20.17). All had been enrolled in full-time day care since early infancy (M = 3.09 months) and, at the time of the study, continued to be enrolled in nonmaternal care on a full-time basis (M = 40.1 hours per week).

Procedure. The subjects were observed in the Strange Situation procedure and classified in accordance with the standard classification scheme specified by Ainsworth, Blehar, Waters, and Wall (1978). Two raters who had received training in scoring the procedure at the University of Minnesota Institute for Child Development scored all of the videotapes independently, with an interrater reliability of 87 percent for major classifications prior to consensus. The coders were blind to subjects' scores on other procedures administered in conjunction with the study.

The Family Environment Scale (FES) (Moos and Moos, 1981) was used to assess the family climate. Mothers rated their marriages on the Dyadic Adjustment Scale (Spanier, 1976). In addition, because parental attitudes can moderate children's attachment security, a parenting questionnaire was used to assess stress and satisfaction in parenting. The parenting questionnaire was composed of a score for stress in the parental role, a protocol developed by Pearlin and Schooler (1978), and a scale measuring mothers' attitudes about their children and their performance in the parental role, using nine items from the Cleminshaw-Guidubaldi Parent Satisfaction Scale (Cleminshaw and Guidubaldi, 1980).

Mothers were also each given a structured interview regarding various aspects of their children's day-care experience. These interviews were conducted subsequent to the completion of all measures. The interview included questions on the child's history of nonmaternal care and on the parents' current perceptions and involvement with their child's day-care center. The interviewers were blind to child attachment classifications as well as to subject scores on other measures.

Results. Out of forty-one subjects, 23 (53.6 percent) were classified as securely attached (B), 13 (31.7 percent) were classified as insecure-avoidant (A), and 6 (14.6 percent) were classified as insecure-resistant (C). Analyses were performed combining the A and C classifications into a single insecure group.

The characteristics of these children's families, as measured on the FES, were related to attachment classifications. Together, five scales were significant predictors in the discriminant-function equation: cohesion, conflict, independence, intellectual-cultural orientation, and organization [Wilkes $\lambda = .69$, χ_2 (5) = 13.49, $p < .01$]. Using this equation, 70.73 percent of the attachment classifications could be correctly classified as A, B, or C. As indicated in Table 3, securely attached children came from families characterized by greater cohesion and greater intellectual-cultural orientation, while insecurely attached children came from families characterized by less conflict, greater independence, and greater organization. Individual analyses of variance revealed that only the differences in level of conflict ($p < .04$) and in intellectual-cultural orientation ($p < .05$) reached statistical significance; there was a trend for cohesion ($p < .09$).

Two multivariate analyses of variance were performed, one on the parenting measures (parenting stress and parenting satisfaction) and the other on the Marital Adjustment Inventory. Both failed to reveal significant differences between the secure and the insecure attachment groups.

Interview Data. A series of t-tests were run to compare the interview

**Table 3. Descriptive Statistics for Family Environment Scale
and Security of Attachment**

	Secure		Insecure		
	Mean	SD	Mean	SD	p
Cohesion*	61.43	7.85	55.83	13.05	ns
Expressiveness	58.65	8.67	53.55	15.50	ns
Conflict*	51.21	9.80	44.77	9.61	p < .04
Independence*	49.95	11.13	52.33	13.23	ns
Achievement orientation	48.47	11.18	52.61	9.43	ns
Intellectual-cultural orientation*	52.21	10.18	45.44	11.27	p < .05
Active-recreational orientation	45.65	12.25	42.05	11.69	ns
Moral-religious emphasis	52.78	9.18	56.77	9.89	ns
Organization*	51.08	12.57	56.00	8.91	ns
Control	47.04	10.39	50.05	12.67	ns

Note: ns = nonsignificant. The five subscales marked with an asterisk were entered together into the discriminant-function equation.

responses of mothers of securely attached children with those of mothers of insecurely attached children. Mothers of securely attached infants were significantly more likely to volunteer at their children's day-care centers (p < .03) and to have been involved in meetings with their children's caregivers (p < .01). There was a trend for mothers of securely attached infants to rate their relationships with their children's caregivers more positively (p < .07).

Mothers of insecurely attached children reported that their children spent more time in one-to-one play activity with fathers (p < .01).

No differences were found between secure and insecure attachment groups on maternal reports of frequency of mothers' contact with caregivers, children's greeting responses when picked up, mothers' feelings when first placing their children in day care, children's current feelings about being in day care, mothers' current feelings about day care, children's ages when first placed in day care, hours in day care, or number of prior day-care arrangements.

In sum, in this second study securely attached children tended to come from families characterized by greater cohesion, but also by greater conflict. In addition, they tended to have mothers who had more contact with their respective day-care centers when compared with mothers of insecurely attached children.

Discussion

The day-care infant's social ecology is quite complex. Long hours in a day-care setting with numerous other infants and at least one caregiver constitute a multilayered context that the infant must integrate over the course of early development. Similarly, the family context for the day-care infant also has a particular set of characteristics, such as the daily separations and reunions and the compressed opportunities to interact with parents; these are added to the standard variables that affect all children's development, such as parental competence and other qualities of the family environment. The two studies reported here were designed to examine elements of both of these major developmental contexts of the day-care child's social ecology as well as the linkages between them.

The concordance between infant-mother and infant-caregiver attachment classifications in the first study, wherein 76 percent of the children had the same attachment classification to mother and caregiver, suggests some potential carry-over effect or generalization from infant-mother attachment security to the infant-caregiver relationship. Prior reports of the infant-mother and infant-caregiver relationships point to a diluted or "intermediate" attachment to (stable) caregivers as opposed to mothers (see Cummings, 1980; and Ainslie and Anderson, 1984).

Infants whose mothers were rated as high in their involvement with the day-care centers were more likely to be securely attached to both their mothers and their caregivers. This was also true, although to a lesser extent, of infants with fathers who were rated as high in their involvement with their children's day-care centers. Especially noteworthy is the fact that *all* of the children whose mothers and fathers were rated as high in their involvement with the day-care centers were found to be securely attached to both their mothers and their caregivers.

Similar results were found in the second study, in which extent of mothers' involvement in their children's day-care settings was significantly related to security of attachment. Thus, in both studies quality of parental involvement with the day-care setting was consistently associated with security of attachment. This may represent an index of parental competence, with more effective parents being more engaged in their children's world, including day care. The consistency of these results across the two studies suggests that parental involvement with the day-care setting is an important variable. Certainly, this interpretation is in keeping with Benn's (1986) and Plunkett's (1980) data on associations between parental competence, quality of child care selected, and quality of parental involvement in child care.

The first study revealed no significant association between the quality of infant-caregiver interactions and the infant-mother or infant-caregiver attachment classifications. The relatively small sample size and considerable variation in the number of infant-caregiver interactions may account for this finding. It is noteworthy, and somewhat surprising, that caregivers rated insecure-avoidant infants most positively on the Infant Characteristics Scales. These infants would be expected to be the least overly dependent in their interactions. The fact that these infants require comparatively less attention may account for this finding. This interpretation is supported by the fact that within the Physicality category, children classified as avoidant with their caregivers had the lowest mean scores for touch (A = 8.7, B = 9.3, C = 13) and for hold (A = 2.1, B = 4.5, C = 3.1), although these differences were not statistically significant. Sample size may be a factor here as well.

The family environment data from the second study did not produce consistent results. A number of subscales from the FES did discriminate between the secure and insecure attachment groups, which suggests that family variables may be important moderators of security of attachment. The higher levels of cohesion in the secure group are in keeping with what one would expect theoretically. That is, families that have a stronger and more positive sense of connection between members may be more likely to foster healthy attachment relationships. However, the higher levels of conflict in the secure group run counter to expectation. It is unclear why this would be the case, unless relatively greater efforts to address needs within the family result in more competent parenting, and at the same time lead parents to feel greater stress. Alternatively, perhaps the greater conflict in the securely attached families is related to greater ambivalence of these mothers about working during their children's first year of life. This would be consistent with Everson, Sarnat, and Ambron (1984), who found that mothers who had experienced the most conflict in placing their children in day care during the first year were more likely to have children who were securely attached. This being the case, one might have expected significant differences in reports of parenting stress and parenting satisfaction between the families with securely attached children and those with insecurely attached children. However, these two instruments differ from the conflict subscale of the FES in important ways, since the parenting stress and parenting satisfaction measures speak directly to the tasks of parenting, while the FES taps a more general tone within the family setting as a whole. It may also be the case that there were differences in these families in terms of their willingness to describe accurately the degree of conflict that they experienced in their family environments.

The design of these two studies does not permit definitive conclusions regarding the interactions between the day-care child's two primary social ecologies, the home and the day-care center. Nevertheless, there is some evidence that home variables play a more important role for the development of attachment. Few center-based variables differentiated the secure from the insecure groups. It is important to note again that the subjects in these two studies attended day-care centers that were judged to be of good quality and were comparable (utilizing the same criteria) in terms of setting characteristics, caregiver-to-child ratio, and philosophy. The children in both studies had been in full-time day care since infancy and at the time of data collection attended the same number of hours. In addition, these centers all met state licensing requirements. It is perhaps not surprising that in day-care centers of good quality the observations of infant-caregiver interactions did not appear to be related to security of attachment. There were no significant differences among caregivers in terms of their overall levels of interaction with the children in their care.

The findings from these two studies provide conflicting evidence for the question of whether enrollment in full-time nonmaternal care during the first year of life poses a risk factor. In the first study, the distribution of attachment classifications is very much in keeping with that reported by Ainsworth, Blehar, Waters, and Wall (1978) and by other researchers with middle-class samples. In the second study, the incidence of both insecure-resistant attachments and insecure-avoidant attachments are somewhat elevated. These latter results replicate those reported by other researchers who have found heightened insecure-resistant and/or insecure-avoidant attachments among children in full-time nonmaternal care during infancy (Vaughn, Gove, and Egeland, 1980; Barglow, Vaughn and Molitor, 1987; Belsky and Rovine, 1988; Belsky, 1988). It bears noting again that these children were enrolled in day-care centers judged to be of good quality, a fact that would obviously dilute potential deleterious effects. In addition, other child care settings may differ in important ways from the centers that participated in these two studies, thereby affecting the nature of their contribution to the day-care child's development. Only approximately 15 percent of day-care children are enrolled in centers, as opposed to family day care or in-home child care (Clarke-Stewart and Gruber, 1984).

In an increasing number of studies (including the second study reported here), there is evidence of increased levels of insecure attachment among children who have been in full-time nonmaternal care since infancy. The results of the present two studies suggest that, in child care of reasonably good quality, home variables may be more important than center variables in moderating security of attachment. Clearly, more research is needed to clarify the nature of differential risk levels in children who are placed in full-time day care since infancy. It is too early to arbitrate definitively among the conflicting perspectives on the effects of early day care. Methodological problems abound. Most studies do not examine variations in day-care quality. Longitudinal data are scarce. Furthermore, studies have varied considerably in the types of day-care settings studied, the ages of entry of children into day care, daily hours in day care, quality of child care employed, and parental attitudes toward child care. This is only a limited list of variables that contribute to the character of a child's day-care experience and thus to the possible effects of such experience on the child's development. We must continue to search for methods and analyses that adequately model the complex social ecology of the young child in day care.

References

Ainslie, R. C., and Anderson, C. W. "Day Care Children's Relationships to Their Mothers and Caregivers: An Inquiry into the Conditions for the Development of

Attachment." In R. C. Ainslie (ed.), *The Child and the Day Care Setting: Qualitative Variations and Development.* New York: Praeger, 1984.

Ainsworth, M.D.S., Blehar, M. C., Waters, E., and Wall, S. *Patterns of Attachment: A Psychological Study of the Strange Situation.* New York: Wiley, 1978.

Barglow, P., Vaughn, B. E., and Molitor, N. "Effects of Maternal Absence Due to Employment on the Quality of Infant-Mother Attachment in a Low-Risk Sample." *Child Development,* 1987, *58,* 945–954.

Belsky, J. "The Effects of Infant Day Care Reconsidered." *Early Childhood Research Quarterly,* 1988, *3,* 235–272.

Belsky, J., and Rovine, M. "Nonmaternal Care in the First Year of Life and Infant-Parent Attachment Security." *Child Development,* 1988, *59,* 157–167.

Benn, R. "Factors Promoting Secure Attachment Relationships Between Employed Mothers and Their Sons." *Child Development,* 1986, *57,* 1224–1231.

Clarke-Stewart, K. A., and Gruber, C. P. "Day Care Forms and Features." In R. C. Ainslie (ed.), *The Child and the Day Care Setting: Qualitative Variations and Development.* New York: Praeger, 1984.

Cleminshaw, H., and Guidubaldi, J. *Assessing Parental Satisfaction.* ERIC No. ED200 858, Oct. 1980.

Cummings, E. M. "Caregiver Stability and Day Care." *Developmental Psychology,* 1980, *16,* 31–37.

Everson, M. D., Sarnat, L., and Ambron, S. R. "Day Care and Early Socialization: The Role of Maternal Attitude." In R. C. Ainslie (ed.), *The Child and the Day Care Setting: Qualitative Variations and Development.* New York: Praeger, 1984.

Farber, E. A., and Egeland, B. "Developmental Consequences of Out-of-Home Care for Infants in a Low-Income Population." In E. F. Zigler and E. W. Gordon (eds.), *Day Care: Scientific and Social Policy Issues.* Boston: Auburn House, 1982.

Howes, C., and Rubenstein, J. L. "Determinants of Toddlers' Experience in Day Care: Age of Entry and Quality of Setting." *Child Care Quarterly,* 1985, *14,* 140–151.

Jacobson, A. L., and Owen, S. S. "Infant-Caregiver Interactions in Day Care." *Child Study Journal,* 1987, *17,* 197–209.

McCartney, K., Scarr, S., Phillips, D., Grajek, S., and Schwarz, J. C. "Environmental Differences Among Day Care Centers and Their Effects on Children's Development." In E. F. Zigler and E. W. Gordon (eds.), *Day Care: Scientific and Social Policy Issues.* Boston: Auburn House, 1982.

Moos, R., and Moos, B. *Family Environment Scale Manual.* Palo Alto, Calif.: Consulting Psychologists Press, 1981.

Pearlin, L., and Schooler, C. "The Structure of Coping." *Journal of Health and Social Behavior,* 1978, *19* (1), 2–21.

Peterson, C., and Peterson, R. "Parent-Child Interaction and Daycare: Does Quality of Daycare Matter?" *Journal of Applied Developmental Psychology,* 1986, *7,* 1–15.

Phillips, D., McCartney, K., Scarr, S., and Howes, C. "Selective Review of Infant Day Care Research: A Cause for Concern?" *Zero to Three,* 1987, *7* (3), 18–21.

Plunkett, M. "Working Mothers of Young Children: A Study of Conflict and Integration." Unpublished doctoral dissertation, Department of Psychology, University of Michigan, 1980.

Spanier, G. B. "Measuring Dyadic Adjustment: New Scales for Assessing the Quality of Marriage and Similar Dyads." *Journal of Marriage and the Family,* 1976, *38,* 15–28.

Stith, S. M., and Davis, A. J. "Employed Mothers and Family Day-Care Substitute Caregivers: A Comparative Analysis of Infant Care." *Child Development,* 1984, *55,* 1340–1348.

Vaughn, B., Gove, F. L., and Egeland, B. "The Relationship Between Out-of-Home Care and the Quality of Infant-Mother Attachment in an Economically Disadvantaged Population." *Child Development,* 1980, *51,* 1203–1214.

Zaslow, M. J., Pedersen, F. A., Suwalsky, J.T.D., Cain, R. L., and Fivel, M. "The Early Resumption of Employment by Mothers: Implications for Parent-Infant Interaction." *Journal of Applied Developmental Psychology*, 1985, *6*, 1–16.

Ricardo C. Ainslie is an associate professor in the Department of Educational Psychology at the University of Texas, Austin.

Mothers' concern about separation is an important moderator
of the effects of maternal employment and child care on children's
development.

Maternal Moderators
of Child Care: The Role of
Maternal Separation Anxiety

Susan L. McBride

If current trends continue, two-thirds of preschool children will have
employed mothers by 1995 (Hofferth and Phillips, 1987). The rise in
employment for mothers of very young children and the resulting increase
in the use of child care have fostered an interest in research that exam-
ines the independent and interactional influences of families and child
care systems on children's development (Phillips and Howes, 1987). With
few exceptions (see Everson, Sarnat, and Ambron, 1984; Hock, DeMeis,
and McBride, 1987), the consideration of maternal psychological well-
being, in general, and of mothers' attitudes about leaving their infants on
a daily basis, in particular, is absent from this research. Mothers express a
wide range of responses when asked how they feel about leaving their
infants or young children for brief separations. Although some women are
not concerned about leaving their children in nonmaternal care, others
dread the thought of being away from their children and often change
their plans to avoid separation. These individual differences represent the
extremes of a continuum of responses to a psychological construct characterized by Hock, McBride, and Gnezda (1989) as *maternal separation
anxiety*. They define maternal separation anxiety as an unpleasant emotional state tied to separation experiences and evidenced by expressions
of worry, sadness, or guilt (1989, p. 794). This chapter discusses the

The author acknowledges Wheelock College for supporting this study and Cathy
Henson and Kathleen Fitzgerald for assistance in data collection.

nature of maternal separation anxiety and its relation to maternal employment and child care patterns.

Maternal Separation Anxiety

The construct of maternal separation anxiety is complex and multidimensional; it no doubt has multiple determinants. Theoretical support for the phenomenon comes from a broad range of perspectives, including the clinically based, psychoanalytic orientation in the work of Benedek (1970) and Mahler, Pine, and Bergman (1975); the ethological theory of attachment advanced by Bowlby (1969); and the ethnic and cultural context of mother-child separations in the work of Frankel and Roer-Bornstein (1982). Some anxiety about separation is normal and desired for the protection and socioemotional development of the child. However, the psychoanalytic tradition suggests that for some mothers, maladaptive early experiences may intensify their need to hold a child close and may hamper their ability to encourage their children's independence. Mothers' feelings are also influenced by cultural expectations and the availability and quality of nonmaternal care. Despite the women's movement and the fact that it is now common for a mother of a young child to be employed, traditional attitudes toward motherhood, particularly the belief in exclusive maternal care for infants, continue to be well rooted in our society (Lauer, 1985; Hock, Gnezda, and McBride, 1984). This has created a situation where women's current participation in the labor force and traditional American values are at odds (McCartney and Phillips, 1988). Many mothers are returning to work in a climate of ambivalence and without the support of social policies or adequate availability of quality child care. These conditions contribute to a mother's feelings about separation from her infant and to her perceptions of the effects of separation on her child. The phenomenon of maternal separation anxiety is now being studied with a new measure, the Maternal Separation Anxiety Scale. In the following review, the scale is described, psychometrics are reported, and maternal correlates and child determinants are discussed.

A Measure of Maternal Separation Anxiety. Hock, McBride, and Gnezda (1989) developed a thirty-five-item questionnaire to measure maternal separation anxiety. The Maternal Separation Anxiety Scale (MSAS) has three subscales that are interpreted and labeled as follows:

Subscale 1: Maternal Separation Anxiety. This subscale includes twenty-one items that reflect general aspects of maternal anxiety and feelings of guilt resulting from or in anticipation of leaving a child. Examples of items include the following: "When I am away from my child, I feel lonely and miss him/her a great deal" and "I like to have my child close to me most of the time."

Subscale 2: Perception of Separation Effects on the Child. This subscale includes seven items that reflect maternal attitudes and feelings about a child's ability to adapt to and profit from nonmaternal care. Examples of items are the following: "Exposure to many different people is good for my child" and "There are times in the lives of young children when they need to be with people other than mothers."

Subscale 3: Employment-Related Separation Concerns. This subscale contains seven items that assess maternal concerns about employment and work-related separations. Items included in this scale are the following: "I would resent my job if it meant I had to be away from my child" and "I would not regret postponing my career in order to stay home with my child."

Psychometric Data from Maternal Separation Anxiety Scale. Several studies have investigated the nature of maternal separation anxiety over time. In an initial study of maternal separation anxiety in the maternity ward and at three months postpartum, Hock, McBride, and Gnezda (1989) found that the three subscales of the MSAS were stable. Subsequent studies have revealed similar findings over longer periods of time, with coefficients ranging from .52 to .72 (McBride and Belsky, 1988; Hock, DeMeis, and McBride, 1987). Pitzer (1984) administered the MSAS to forty mothers when their first-borns were seven months old, and again to the same mothers when their second-borns were seven months old. The stability coefficients were moderate. These findings suggest that the mothers who were most likely to be anxious when their infants were young were also most likely to be anxious later, even with a second child. Thus, maternal separation anxiety seems to be a rather stable personality characteristic. Although there is considerable consistency for individuals over time, specific characteristics of a situation may heighten or lower levels of maternal separation anxiety, such as characteristics of the mother or the child.

Maternal Correlates. The relationship between maternal separation anxiety and other aspects of personality has been given some consideration. Hock, McBride, and Gnezda (1989) found that maternal separation anxiety was moderately correlated with a measure of manifest anxiety. This suggests that anxiety about separation is related to levels of general anxiety, but the modest coefficient implies that separation anxiety is a unique phenomenon with a significant portion of the variance accounted for by other variables. McBride and Belsky (1988) found that women with lower levels of self-esteem and higher levels of interpersonal affect expressed greater maternal separation anxiety. They suggest that mothers who are more sensitive to interpersonal affect may have higher separation anxiety as a result of being more sensitive to the feelings of their infants. The proper interpretation of the relationship to low self-esteem is not clear. Women with low self-esteem may be less confident about parenting and express more concern about leaving their children, while women with high self-esteem may have a tendency to defend or deny concern about separation. These findings suggest that maternal separation anxiety may be related to basic personality characteristics. However, since personality is an expression of the interaction between the person and situation, factors related to balancing motherhood and employment may have an impact on levels of maternal separation anxiety.

In this regard, mothers' concerns about separation have been associated with variables related to role satisfaction such as maternal role investment and career orientation. Gnezda (1983) found that women who expressed greater separation anxiety were more invested in the maternal role and less career oriented. Of particular interest was the fact that these associations held for women who were subsequently employed as well as for those who were not; thus, these statistical associations were not simply a function of mean differences in the separation anxiety expressed by mothers in and out of the paid labor force. However, the psychological experiences of these two groups of mothers cannot be assumed to be equivalent with regard to separation anxiety. Evidence of differences as a function of employment preference comes from two other studies.

In a study designed to investigate how older, well-educated mothers come to terms with balancing maternal and career roles over the first year of motherhood, DeMeis, Hock, and McBride (1986) found that maternal separation anxiety is related to both the mother's preference to be employed or at home with her child and her actual employment status. They compared a group of mothers who preferred to be employed with a group who preferred to be at home caring for their infants. Over the first year of their children's lives, the level of general maternal separation anxiety (subscale 1) for all mothers decreased. Although the scores of the two groups were similar on subscale 1 at two days and seven weeks, employment-preference mothers had significantly lower scores than did home-preference mothers by eight and thirteen-and-one-half months. When the actual work status of the home-preference group was considered, employed mothers who preferred home had lower scores than nonemployed mothers on subscale 3, employment-related separation concerns at two days and thirteen-and-one-half months. With a larger, more diverse sample, Hock, DeMeis, and McBride (1987) found mothers who preferred to be employed expressed lower levels of anxiety on all three subscales of the MSAS. A more complicated effect of time-by-preference-by-employment-status was significant for employment-related separation concerns (subscale 3).

Both of these studies indicate that the relative importance of work and motherhood may change for mothers over time. Work preference is a strong indicator of maternal separation anxiety, but levels of maternal separation anxiety after early infancy may adjust to consistency with actual work status. It is likely that those mothers who preferred to be home became more convinced over time that separation, for the purpose of employment, is undesirable. For those who were employed, either the employment experience reduced maternal anxiety or mothers repressed their anxiety to reduce dissonance between their preference and actual behavior. Thus, maternal concerns about separation are not static, and mothers form attitudes that are consistent with a balance between motherhood and employment. If this is the case, it is also likely that characteristics of the mother's job and the type and quality of the care setting for her child are important factors influencing the integration of motherhood and employment. The study presented later in this chapter was designed to provide some insight into the relationships between characteristics of maternal employment, child care, and maternal separation anxiety.

Child Determinants. An interactional, if not transactional, model of development would predict that characteristics of children also have an influence on individual levels of maternal separation anxiety. There are indications that the variables of age, temperament, gender, and birth order of children are related to differences in maternal separation anxiety. To summarize the longitudinal data described above, as children get older, mothers' absolute levels of maternal separation anxiety decrease. Although age interacts with other characteristics of maternal employment, such as employment preference and employment status, it is also likely that mothers perceive their very young infants as vulnerable but, over time, realize that the infants are able to cope with routine separations.

McBride and Belsky (1988) provide evidence that infant gender and temperament are related to differences in maternal separation anxiety. With employment-related separation anxiety (subscale 3), they found a significant time-by-gender interaction. The scores of mothers of girls decreased from three to nine months, while those of mothers of boys increased. The researchers suggest that this finding may reflect a perceived heightened vulnerability of males to nonmaternal care. They cite findings from a related study indicating that mothers who planned to be employed following their infants' births were more likely not to do so if they had boys, whereas mothers who expected to stay at home but who returned to work were more likely to have given birth to girls (Volling and Belsky, 1987). In this same study, temperament-related findings were consistent with the notion that infants with problematical temperaments (more dull and unpredictable) had mothers who were reportedly more anxious about separation. In a study of infants with and without colic, Humphry (1985) found that mothers of colicky babies had significantly higher levels of general maternal separation anxiety (subscale 1). Thus, babies who are perceived to be vulnerable may elicit greater concern about separation. Birth order also appears to be an important correlate. Although the relative amount of anxiety expressed by mothers of first- and second-borns is stable, mothers expressed less anxiety with the second child (Pitzer, 1984).

In summary, recent studies reveal that maternal separation anxiety is a complex phenomenon with multiple correlates. Characteristics of both mothers (their work situation and personality) and infants (gender, age, temperament, birth order) are related to individual differences in maternal separation anxiety.

Consequences. Researchers have only started to explore the consequences of maternal separation anxiety for children and their mothers. In a study designed to validate the MSAS, Hock, McBride, and Gnezda (1989) found that levels of maternal separation anxiety were related to ratings of maternal behavior. Higher levels of maternal separation anxiety were associated with anxious maternal behaviors such as soothing a nondistressed child, questioning the caregiver extensively about the child's behavior, or asking their infants if they missed them. Mothers who expressed higher levels of maternal separation anxiety also lingered in the lab, after being told that they could leave, in order to continue to interact with their children and to reassure themselves that everything was alright. Another study has also linked maternal separation anxiety and maternal behavior. Berger and Aber (1986) found that higher scores on the MSAS were associated with maternal behaviors that reflected less support for autonomy in their toddlers. These findings suggest that high levels of maternal separation anxiety may interfere with age-appropriate patterns of mothering or may be linked to intrusive mothering. Because these patterns of mothering have been associated with nonsecure attachment relationships, the findings warrant concern (see Isabella, Belsky, and Von Eye, 1989).

These studies also raise the question of what is the most desirable level of maternal separation anxiety. Both theory and research indicate that there may be an optimal amount of maternal separation anxiety. From clinical observations Benedek (1970) proposed that both high and low levels of anxiety can be emotionally handicapping and interfere with appropriate mothering. She noted that mothers who experience no separation anxiety do not cathect their infants with the intensity of emotions considered to be normal in our culture and, as a result, may never become attached to their infants. At the other end of the continuum, heightened separation anxiety may result in overprotective behavior that interferes with individuation.

In order to examine the potential consequences of levels of maternal separation anxiety, McBride and Belsky (1988) examined the scores of the three subscales of the MSAS with infant-mother attachment security. Only in the case of employment-related separation anxiety (subscale 3) was there a significant difference in the three attachment groups (secure, insecure-avoidant, and insecure-resistant). Mothers of secure infants expressed the most employment-related separation anxiety, and more so than the combined groups of insecure infants. The correlation between general separation anxiety (subscale 1) and security of attachment was marginally significant, with the same mothers of secure infants expressing a moderate degree of general separation anxiety: less than mothers of avoidant infants but more than mothers of resistant ones. These results suggest that moderate levels of general separation anxiety and higher levels of employment-related separation anxiety may be optimal for mothers to be sensitive to their children's experience and relate to them in particularly sensitive and security-promoting ways. If employed, these mothers may also be more oriented toward and skilled in obtaining high-quality care for their children. Consistent with this line of thinking is evidence that maternal separation anxiety is systematically related to the quality of care that mothers use.

Hock, DeMeis, and McBride (1987) reported findings from a longitudinal study of maternal separation anxiety where data related to choices in child care were available. The sample consisted of 107 mothers: 73 had been steadily employed over the first three years of their children's lives and 34 had been at home. The employed mothers who enrolled their infants in day-care centers instead of using baby-sitters or family day-care homes expressed significantly lower levels of separation anxiety related to the perception of the effects of separation on their children (subscale 2). In addition, among those mothers who used day-care centers, mothers who expressed more anxiety about balancing motherhood and employment (subscale 3) used this type of care fewer months over the three-year period. A second analysis considered the use of preschool at age three. Surprisingly, only 16 percent of the children of nonemployed mothers (compared to 58 percent of the employed mothers) had children enrolled in a group that met at least three half-days a week. When the number of half-days of preschool attendance was correlated with the MSAS, separation anxiety related to effects on the child (subscale 2) was associated with less-frequent use of preschool for children of nonemployed mothers but not for children of employed mothers.

Given the many factors that can influence preschool attendance, the relationship between maternal separation anxiety and enrollment in preschool is important. These findings suggest that a woman who is highly anxious about separation may select a different type of child care than a woman who is less anxious. What is not yet known is whether maternal separation anxiety plays a role in the quality of care that mothers choose for their children. However, the studies of maternal separation anxiety do suggest that outcomes for children may be a result of parental attitudes, beliefs, and emotions instead of or in addition to interactions with maternal employment status and use of nonmaternal care.

A Study of Maternal Separation Anxiety, Mothers' Employment, and Quality of Child Care

The following study was designed to investigate the relationships between characteristics of maternal separation anxiety, mothers' employment, and quality of child care. Four specific research questions were proposed: (1) Is there a relationship between mothers' employment patterns and maternal separation anxiety? (2) Are occupational characteristics of the job related to levels of maternal separation anxiety? (3) Does maternal separation anxiety play a role in the selection of type of child care setting? And (4) is maternal separation anxiety associated with the dynamic or the structural components of the quality of the child care setting?

Sample. The sample for this study consisted of forty-nine mothers of children two-to-three years of age, attending eighteen different day-care centers in a large metropolitan area in the northeast United States. The day-care centers were also sites for a larger study, the National Child Care Staffing Study (NCCSS) (Whitebook, Howes, and Phillips, 1989). A stratified random-sampling procedure was used to select centers, assuring equal representation between urban versus suburban and profit versus nonprofit centers.

Recruitment. Thirty centers that offered programs for infants and toddlers and were target centers in the national study were contacted for this study. All but one of these centers agreed to assist in recruiting families to participate in the present study. Center directors were asked to identify families who fit the criteria for eligibility: two-parent, English-speaking families with children ranging in age from eighteen to thirty-six months who were in classrooms observed for the NCCSS project. Sixty-nine families returned the consent forms and were contacted by telephone and given more information about what their participation in this study would entail. Ninety-one percent ($N = 63$) of those contacted agreed to participate in the study. A telephone interview was conducted with mothers of these families and questionnaires were sent to both parents to return by mail. The final sample consisted of 78 percent of those families who were interviewed where at least the mother returned her questionnaire ($N = 49$).

Description of Sample. The sample consisted primarily of Caucasian, well-educated, two-income, upper-middle-class families. The average age of mothers in this study wa 34.6 years (range: 26–43 years) and all were married. All mothers had completed high school and the mean level of education included some study beyond an undergraduate degree. The mean family income was $51,000 (range: $31,000–$75,000). At the time of the study, all mothers were employed, 82 percent full-time (more than thirty hours per week) and 18 percent part-time. On average, mothers returned to work 4 weeks after the births of their children (range: 4–48 weeks). The age of the children ranged from 17 months to 47 months ($M = 27.69$); 63 percent were boys and 37 percent were second-born children.

Method and Measures. As noted above, the data for this study were collected through telephone interviews with the mothers and questionnaires that were completed and returned by mail. Each interview, from twenty to thirty minutes in duration, provided demographic information about the family, characteristics of the mother's employment (type of occupation, age of child when mother returned to work, number of hours employed per week), and details on the mother's perceptions of both the difficulty in finding child care and the criteria used to select a child care center. The mothers also responded verbally to scales that assessed their perceptions of job characteristics (see description below). The MSAS was one of several measures included in the questionnaire that was returned by mail, but the only measure analyzed in this study. The data on quality of care were collected by the project staff of the NCCSS. Table 1 provides descriptive statistics for the study variables.

Maternal Job Characteristics. Psychosocial job characteristics were measured by four scales. Job demands was the extent to which the job required physical or mental exertion from the respondent. It was assessed by a four-item index based on items developed by Karasek (1979). Respondents were asked to answer questions about the pressure of work load and pace. Job autonomy was defined as the possibility for an employee to exercise control over his or her job tasks and the organizational policies that affect the job (Piotrowski and Katz, 1982). It was assessed by a four-item scale that tapped task independence and closeness of supervision. Supervisor support was defined as the extent to which the respondent perceived her supervisor to be supportive, flexible, and understanding of her family responsibilities. The eight items in this scale are a combination of items based on work by Quinn and Staines (1979) and Hughes and Galinsky (1988). The index of work/psychological spillover was composed of five items that describe the frequency of negative job-related moods such as preoccupation with work, fatigue, and irritability with children (Hughes and Galinsky, 1987). All items were rated on five-point Likert scales.

Table 1. Descriptive Statistics for Study Variables

Variable	N	%	M	SD	Range
Employment					
Hours employed per week	49		37.0	8.7	20–60
Child age when mother returned to work (weeks)	49		16.9	9.4	4–48
Hollingshead occupational status			7.7	1.1	5–9
Sales and clerical	1	2.0			
Technicians	5	10.2			
Managers	18	36.7			
Administrators and lesser professions	9	18.4			
Professionals	16	32.7			

Table 1. (*continued*)

Variable	N	%	M	SD	Range
Job characteristics					
Job demands	49		14.1	3.13	6–20
Job autonomy	49		15.0	2.52	7–20
Supervisor support	45		32.4	5.70	13–40
Work/psychological spillover	49		11.3	2.60	5–17
MSAS					
Maternal separation anxiety	48		18.5	3.74	10–27
Perception of separation effects on child	48		14.6	4.33	7–22
Employment-related separation	48		19.7	4.89	7–30
Selection of child care					
Difficulty locating care	49		2.7	1.34	1–5
Criteria for selecting day-care center					
First:					
Quality of staff	34	70			
Environment	9	18			
Philosophy	6	12			
Second:					
Quality of staff	8	16			
Environment	24	49			
Philosophy	10	20			
Access	7	14			
Quality of care					
Dynamic components					
ECERS					
Caregiving scale	49		4.4	.55	3–5
Environment scale	49		5.1	.75	3–7
Caregiver interaction scale					
Sensitive	41		28.83	5.88	18–37
Harsh	41		13.34	3.84	9–27
Detached	41		6.61	3.09	4–13
Permissive	41		1.17	1.55	-1–4
Structural components					
Adult-child ratio	49		3.3	.99	1.5–7.0
Group size	49		10.0	4.60	3–19

Quality of Child Care Setting. Both structural and dynamic aspects of the quality of child care were assessed. These data were collected through observation in the centers. The Early Childhood Environmental Rating Scale (ECERS) (Harms and Clifford, 1980) was administered at each center by a member of the NCCSS research team after several hours of observation in the center. This scale consists of thirty-eight items judged by early childhood professionals to be extremely important components of quality programs for children and has been shown to have high interrater reliability (McCartney, 1984; Harms and Clifford, 1980). The items are rated on a seven-point scale and focus on seven areas of quality (personal care routines, furnishings and display, language and reasoning experiences, creative activities, fine- and gross-motor activities, social development, and adult needs). Infant items on the test were used for the majority of the centers since the children were in infant and toddler classrooms. In two instances the preschool version of the rating scale was used. The scores from the infant and preschool scales are comparable and were consequently combined. The data collected with this instrument for all centers participating in the NCCSS project were factor-analyzed and yielded two discrete subscales (see Whitebook, Howes, and Phillips, 1989). The two subscales reflect items representative of the quality of caregiving interactions and the quality of the environment. These same subscales were used for the present study.

In addition to the ECERS, the dynamic quality of the centers was also assessed using the Caregiver Interaction Scale (Arnett, in press), which specifically assesses the nature of caregiver-child interactions. This scale consists of twenty-six items rated on a four-point scale. The items in the scale are combined to reflect the presence of four different types of caregiver interactions: sensitive, harsh, detached, and permissive. The data for this scale were also collected by the staff of the NCCSS project after observation in the centers.

The structural dimensions of the quality of care were indicators of adult-child ratios in the classrooms and group size. These data were collected by the staff of the NCCSS through observation and consultation with directors of the programs.

Results. Correlational analyses were conducted to explore the relationship of the variables selected to measure characteristics of maternal employment and child care with maternal separation anxiety. Findings with significance levels of $p < .10$ and lower were included to document trends and patterns.

Maternal Employment Patterns and Maternal Separation Anxiety. As presented in Table 2, the age of the child when mothers in this sample returned to work tended to be related to the mothers' levels of general (subscale 1) and employment-related (subscale 3) maternal separation anxiety. Mothers who expressed higher levels of separation anxiety on the two

**Table 2. Correlations Between Characteristics of
Maternal Employment and Maternal Separation Anxiety**

	Subscale 1 Maternal Separation Anxiety	Subscale 2 Separation Effects on Child	Subscale 3 Employment-Related Separation Anxiety
Hours employed per week	-.11	-.23[b]	-.34[c]
Child age when mother returned to work	.22[a]	.02	.21[a]
Occupational status	.06	.04	-.17
Job characteristics			
Job demands	.28[b]	.19[a]	-.08
Job autonomy	-.21[a]	-.08	-.33[c]
Supervisor support	-.23[a]	-.07	.02
Work/psychological spillover	.31[c]	-.07	.12

[a] $p < .10$
[b] $p < .05$
[c] $p < .01$

subscales returned to work later in the first year of their children's lives. Note that the number of hours that mothers were working was significantly associated with expressions of maternal separation anxiety, with mothers who worked fewer hours per week expressing more separation anxiety related to effects on their children (subscale 2) and employment (subscale 3). Thus, maternal separation anxiety is associated with maternal employment patterns.

Occupational Characteristics and Maternal Separation Anxiety. Occupational status was not related to levels of maternal separation anxiety. However, other occupational characteristics were associated with maternal separation anxiety. Mothers who expressed higher levels of general maternal separation anxiety (subscale 1) reported that they held more highly demanding jobs, that they tended to be in positions in which they felt less autonomous, and that they received less support from their supervisors. Mothers who scored high on subscale 1 also expressed significantly more work/psychological spillover. Mothers' perceptions of separation effects on their children (subscale 2) were marginally related to higher job demands, and increased levels of employment-related separation anxiety (subscale 3) were significantly associated with less job autonomy (see Table 2).

Characteristics of Child Care and Maternal Separation Anxiety. Meaningful relationships were found between maternal separation anxiety and the selection of type of child care (see Table 3). Mothers who expressed higher levels of general separation anxiety (subscale 1) also reported significantly more difficulty in locating child care. In terms of the criteria used to select child care, subscale 2 was most salient. Mothers who expressed

Table 3. Correlations Between Selection of Child Care and Maternal Separation Anxiety

	Subscale 1 Maternal Separation Anxiety	Subscale 2 Separation Effects on Child	Subscale 3 Employment-Related Separation Anxiety
Difficulty locating care	$.38^c$	.05	−.03
Criteria for selecting day-care center			
First:			
Quality of staff	.01	$−.21^a$	−.04
Environment	.08	$.32^c$	.09
Philosophy	.10	−.08	−.06
Second:			
Quality of staff	.03	$.26^b$	.11
Environment	.05	$−.22^a$	−.04
Philosophy	−.01	.16	−.08
Access	−.10	−.16	−.05

[a] $p < .10$
[b] $p < .05$
[c] $p < .01$

higher levels of anxiety related to their perceptions of the effects of separation on their children were significantly more likely to indicate that the physical environment (versus quality of staff) was their first consideration in choosing a center for their children. These mothers also indicated significantly more often that the quality of the staff was their second most-important criterion.

Maternal Separation Anxiety and the Quality of the Child Care Setting. Correlations between variables assessing the quality of care and maternal separation anxiety are presented in Table 4. Subscales 1 and 2 were related to structural components of center quality and subscale 3 was related to dynamic components of quality. Mothers who expressed higher levels of general separation anxiety (subscale 1) and anxiety related to the effects of separation on the child (subscale 2) had children in classrooms with lower adult-child ratios. Mothers who expressed more employment-related separation anxiety (subscale 3) were more likely to have children in lower-quality centers, that is, centers with lower ratings on the environmental factor of the ECERS and where caregiver interactions were scored as being less sensitive and more harsh.

Discussion and Conclusions

This study was designed to further our understanding of the relationship between maternal separation anxiety, maternal employment, and child care patterns. The findings suggest that characteristics of mothers' occupations

Table 4. Correlations Between Quality of Care and Maternal Separation Anxiety

	Subscale 1 Maternal Separation Anxiety	Subscale 2 Separation Effects on Child	Subscale 3 Employment-Related Separation Anxiety
Dynamic components			
ECERS			
Caregiving scale	-.10	-.09	-.02
Environment scale	-.16	.03	-.24[b]
Caregiver interaction scale			
Sensitive	-.16	-.09	-.28[b]
Harsh	-.09	.07	.26[b]
Detached	.12	.01	.11
Permissive	-.05	.02	-.04
Structural components			
Adult-child ratio	-.22[a]	-.38[c]	-.04
Group size	-.02	-.03	-.16

[a] $p < .1$
[b] $p < .05$
[c] $p < .01$

are associated with maternal separation anxiety. The study also revealed that mothers' concerns about separation are related to their decisions about child care, for example, when they return to work and the criteria they use to select care for their children. An important finding was the relationship between the quality of the day-care center and mothers' levels of maternal separation anxiety.

This study is the first to explore the relationship between characteristics of women's jobs and their levels of separation anxiety. The findings suggest that although the type of occupation held by each mother in this sample was not associated with maternal separation anxiety, specific psychosocial characteristics of the job were related. This study does not, however, provide insight into whether a difficult work situation, for example, one that is highly demanding and provides less autonomy or has less supervisor support for family demands, increases mothers' levels of anxiety about leaving their children or whether mothers who are already concerned about leaving their children perceive their work situations as difficult. There may be a transactional relationship between these two sets of variables. Alternatively, a third variable such as career orientation or investment in the mother role may influence both sets of variables. A longitudinal study that includes these variables is needed to ascertain the direction of these relationships.

The importance of maternal separation anxiety to the child's experience with nonmaternal care is suggested by the findings related to the timing of the resumption of employment and the amount of time per week children are in day care. Although all mothers in this sample returned to work before their children were one year of age, those who reported lower levels of general and employment-related maternal separation anxiety (subscales 1 and 3) when their children were ages two to three had returned to work earlier. Again, the direction of the relationship is not clear. Mothers who are less concerned about being away from their infants may find it easier to return to employment when their infants are quite young. It is also likely that specific occupational situations, characteristics of the children, and the availability of child care are factors that influence when mothers return to their jobs. Levels of separation anxiety related to effects on the child (subscale 2) and employment (subscale 3) were also negatively related to the current number of hours per week mothers were employed. This finding replicates that of Hock, DeMeis, and McBride (1987), who found that maternal separation anxiety was negatively related to use of child care.

In terms of the process of selecting nonmaternal care, individual subscales of the MSAS appear to measure different aspects of the process. Those mothers who scored higher on general maternal separation anxiety (subscale 1) indicated that they had more difficulty locating child care. For these mothers, concern about leaving their infants may have made this process more difficult or the perceived (or real!) unavailability of care may have heightened their concerns. The latter suggestion is supported by a recent study that found a significant relationship between difficulty in finding child care and depression in employed mothers (Ross and Mirowsky, 1988). Only anxiety related to the perception of the effects of separation on the child (subscale 2) was related to the criteria mothers reported they used to select child care. Overall, mothers participating in this study appeared to understand the important characteristics of quality child care. From open-ended questions, they most often reported the quality of the staff (70 percent) to be their first criterion in selecting centers for their children. Concern for the child care environment was the second most important criterion (49 percent). Although both quality of staff and characteristics of the environment are important components of quality care, it is interesting that mothers who expressed more separation anxiety related to effects on the child (subscale 2) were more likely to report the opposite priorities. They were more likely to name the environment as their first criterion and the quality of staff as their second. This is a somewhat perplexing finding. Perhaps, for these particular mothers, issues of a safe environment were particularly salient.

The most significant findings from this study are the relationships between the components of quality of care and maternal separation anxiety. Mothers who expressed more general separation anxiety (subscale 1) and anxiety about separation effects on their children (subscale 2) had children in classrooms with lower adult-child ratios. Although the direction of effects is not clear, it is likely that more anxious mothers may have purposely selected centers where they felt their children would get more attention. However, more anxiety on either subscales 1 or 2 was not related to other components of quality such as scores on the ECERS and the Caregiver Interaction Scale. Mothers of the children who were in centers that received higher scores on the environment factor of the ECERS and where caregivers were rated as providing more sensitive and less harsh interactions expressed less employment-related separation anxiety. This finding quite likely suggests that high-quality care contributes to the decrease in maternal separation anxiety for employed mothers. What this means for children is not clear. It may be that in early infancy, mothers' anxiety about balancing employment and motherhood serves an important function in providing sensitive mothering and in selecting quality care (McBride and Belsky, 1988). Later, mothers with children in high-quality care may be able to resolve their concerns and more satisfactorily integrate their roles of mother and worker.

It is important to remember that these findings represent a sample of mothers who were primarily working full-time in occupations of high prestige and that their children were in day-care centers that were of adequate or better quality. This restricted range in demographics and quality of care confines the generalizability of the findings. The findings, however, have implications for employment practices and further research.

The relationship between maternal separation anxiety and psychosocial characteristics of the job situation has important implications for women and their employers. Predicted labor force demands will allow women to select employment situations that are most supportive of their efforts to balance work and family responsibilities. To be competitive, the attention of employers should be directed toward eliminating these characteristics of employment that interfere with the quality of family life or the psychological well-being of parents. Hughes and Galinsky (1988) report that lack of supervisor support predicted high levels of stress in mothers of children under eighteen years of age. Mothers in the same study reported more anxiety about leaving their children when their supervisors were less supportive. Sensitizing supervisors to the multiple family and employment-related demands of mothers of young children and providing flexible employment environments may be particularly important tasks for employers to consider.

The findings also suggest that some parents may need more information about the components of high-quality care. Mothers who are very concerned about how their children will adapt to or profit from nonmaternal care may be in particular need of more specific information regarding the relative importance of caregiver-child interactions.

This study also raises several questions that deserve further research. Most clear is the need for longitudinal studies utilizing path analyses to determine the direction of many of the significant relationships found in the present study. Although important research has been conducted that begins to tease out the relative influences and interactions of family and child care variables in relation to outcomes for children (for example, Howes and Olenick, 1986; Phillips, McCartney, and Scarr, 1987; Vandell and Corasaniti, this volume), consideration of the psychological well-being of mothers must be included in future research. Maternal separation anxiety may be one of several important linkages between the family and child care environment and a moderator of the effects of maternal employment and day care on children.

References

Arnett, J. "Caregivers in Day Care Centers: Does Training Matter?" *Journal of Applied Developmental Psychology,* in press.

Benedek, T. "Motherhood and Nurturing." In E. J. Anthony and T. Benedek (eds.), *Parenthood: Its Psychology and Psychopathology.* Boston: Little, Brown, 1970.

Berger, B., and Aber, J. L. "Maternal Autonomy in Separation: A New Measure of Mothers' Negotiating Ability During Separation." Paper presented at the International Conference on Infant Studies, Los Angeles, April 1986.

Bowlby, J. *Attachment and Loss.* Vol. 1. London: Hogarth, 1969.

DeMeis, D. K., Hock, E., and McBride, S. L. "The Balance of Employment and Motherhood: Longitudinal Study of Mothers' Feelings About Separation from Their First-Born Infants." *Developmental Psychology,* 1986, *22,* 627–632.

Everson, M. D., Sarnat, L. T., and Ambron, S. R. "Day Care and Early Socialization: The Role of Maternal Attitude." In R. C. Ainslie (ed.), *The Child and the Day-Care Setting: Qualitative Variations and Development.* New York: Praeger, 1984.

Frankel, D. G., and Roer-Bornstein, D. *Traditional and Modern Contributions to Changing Infant-Rearing Ideologies of Two Ethnic Communities.* Monographs of the Society for Research in Child Development, vol. 47, no. 4 (serial no. 196). Chicago: University of Chicago Press, 1982.

Gnezda, M. T. "The Nature of Maternal Separation Anxiety as It Relates to Employment-Related Separations." Unpublished doctoral dissertation, Department of Family Relations and Human Development, Ohio State University, 1983.

Harms, T., and Clifford, R. M. *Early Childhood Environment Rating Scale.* New York: Teachers College Press, 1980.

Hock, E., DeMeis, D., and McBride, S. "Maternal Separation Anxiety: Its Role in the Balance of Employment and Motherhood in Mothers of Infants." In A. E. Gottfried and A. W. Gottfried (eds.), *Maternal Employment and Children's Development: Longitudinal Research.* New York: Plenum, 1988.

Hock, E., Gnezda, T., and McBride, S. "Mothers of Infants: Attitudes Toward Employment and Motherhood Following Birth of the First Child." *Journal of Marriage and the Family,* May 1984, pp. 425–431.

Hock, E., McBride, S., and Gnezda, T. "Maternal Separation Anxiety: Mother-Infant Separation from the Maternal Perspective." *Child Development,* 1989, *60,* 793–802.

Hofferth, S., and Phillips, D. "Children in the United States, 1970–1995." *Journal of Marriage and the Family,* 1987, *59,* 559–571.

Howes, C., and Olenick, M. "Family and Child Care Influences on Toddlers' Compliance." *Child Development,* 1986, *57,* 202–216.

Hughes, D., and Galinsky, E. "Balancing Work and Family Lives." In A. E. Gottfried and A. W. Gottfried (eds.), *Maternal Employment and Children's Development: Longitudinal Research.* New York: Plenum, 1988.

Humphry, R. A. "Colic in Infancy and the Mother-Infant Relationship." Unpublished doctoral dissertation, Department of Family Relations and Human Development, Ohio State University, 1985.

Isabella, R., Belsky, J., and Van Eye, A. "Origins of Infant-Mother Attachment: An Examination of Interactional Synchrony During the Infant's First Year." *Developmental Psychology,* 1989, *25,* 12–21.

Karasek, R. "Job Demands, Job Decision Latitude, and Mental Strain: Implications for Job Redesign." *Administrative Science Quarterly,* 1979, *24,* 285–308.

Lauer, H. "Jobs in the 1980s: A Sourcebook for Policymakers." In D. Yankelovich, H. Zetterberg, B. Strumpel, and M. Shanks (eds.), *The World at Work.* New York: Octagon Books, 1985.

McBride, S., and Belsky, J. "Characteristics, Determinants, and Consequences of Maternal Separation Anxiety." *Child Development,* 1988, *24,* 407–414.

McCartney, K. "The Effect of Quality of Day Care Environment upon Children's Language Development." *Developmental Psychology,* 1984, *20,* 244–260.

McCartney, K., and Phillips, D. "Motherhood and Child Care." In B. Birns and D. Hay (eds.), *The Different Faces of Motherhood.* New York: Plenum, 1988.

Mahler, M. S., Pine, F., and Bergman, A. *The Psychological Birth of the Human Infant.* New York: Basic Books, 1975.

Phillips, D., and Howes, C. "Quality in Child Care: Review of Research." In D. Phillips (ed.), *Quality in Child Care: What Does Research Tell Us?* Research Monograph of the National Association for the Education of Young Children, vol. 1. Washington, D.C.: National Association for the Education of Young Children, 1987.

Phillips, D., McCartney, K., and Scarr, S. "Child Care Quality and Children's Social Development." *Developmental Psychology,* 1987, *23,* 537–543.

Piotrowski, C., and Katz, M. "Indirect Socialization of Children: The Effects of Mothers' Jobs on Academic Behaviors." *Child Development,* 1982, *53,* 1520–1529.

Pitzer, M. "A Study of Maternal Separation Anxiety in Working Mothers of Second-Born Infants." Unpublished doctoral dissertation, Department of Family Relations and Human Development, Ohio State University, 1984.

Quinn, R., and Staines, G. *The 1977 Quality of Employment Survey: Descriptive Statistics with Comparison Data from 1969–70 and 1972–73 Surveys.* Ann Arbor, Mich.: Institute for Social Research, 1979.

Ross, C., and Mirowsky, J. "Child Care and Emotional Adjustment to Wives' Employment." *Journal of Health and Social Behavior,* 1988, *29,* 127–138.

Volling, B., and Belsky, J. "Demographic, Maternal, and Infant Factors Associated with Maternal Employment in the Infant's First Year of Life." Unpublished manuscript, Department of Human Development and Family Studies, Pennsylvania State University, 1987.

Whitebook, M., Howes, C., and Phillips, D. *Who Cares? Child Care Teachers and the Quality of Care in America.* Executive summary of the National Child Care Staffing Study. Oakland, Calif.: Child Care Employee Project, 1989.

Susan L. McBride is an associate professor in the Department of Human Development and Family Studies, Iowa State University, Ames.

*The current empirical controversy concerning the effects of early
nonmaternal care on the quality of infant-mother attachment is,
in part, the product of fundamental theoretical differences among
researchers.*

Early Nonmaternal Care and Infant
Attachment: In Search of Process

Elizabeth Jaeger, Marsha Weinraub

Research conducted over the span of nearly two decades has not yielded
consistent answers regarding the consequences of nonmaternal care arrangements for very young children. While this issue once left child care
researchers divided (see Belsky, 1986; Phillips, McCartney, Scarr, and
Howes, 1987), it is now prompting an unprecedented collaborative effort
to address this question.

In the hopes of better understanding the developmental implications
of nonmaternal care for infants, the National Center for Clinical Infant
Programs (NCCIP) convened a meeting hosted by the National Academy of
Sciences and the Institute of Medicine in the fall of 1987. At this meeting,
leading child care researchers developed a list of issues to be addressed
(NCCIP, 1988). They recommended that demographic information on the
characteristics, employment experience, and child care arrangements of
families and the characteristics of child care settings be collected, with
special attention to the complex interactions among these variables. They
urged the use of multiple measures to assess all aspects of the family
situation and child care, stressing the importance of ecological validity. In
May 1989, the National Institute of Child Health and Human Development

Portions of this chapter were presented by the second author at the meetings of
the Society for Research in Child Development, April 1989, Kansas City, Missouri.
We are extremely grateful to Peter Comalli, Rob Fauber, Kathleen Hirsh-Pasek,
Nora Newcombe, Willis Overton, Larry Steinberg, Ron Taylor, and Diana Woodruff-
Pak for comments on earlier versions of this chapter, and to Jay Belsky for more
recent comments. Requests for reprints should be addressed to Elizabeth Jaeger,
Department of Psychology, Temple University, Philadelphia, Pennsylvania, 19122.

funded a nationwide collaborative study that is sufficiently comprehensive in scope to address the questions outlined by the NCCIP.

The current focus on measurement issues and the increasing concern with "risk factors"—those factors that can be used to predict developmental outcomes associated with nonmaternal infant care—have, to some extent, diverted attention away from fundamental questions of developmental processes. To design effective child care intervention strategies, researchers must not only identify potential risk factors but also have some insight into the mechanisms and processes by which risk factors are operative. To address questions of process we turn, in this chapter, toward the theories that have been used to understand the processes by which maternal employment affects child outcomes.

With a few notable exceptions (see, for example, McCartney, Scarr, Phillips, Grajek, and Schwarz, 1982; Sroufe, 1988; Thompson, 1988), the role of theory in child care research has been largely overlooked. We believe that differences in the interpretation of data have arisen because of unarticulated theoretical differences underlying the approaches of different researchers. Although researchers are moving toward a consensus on *methodological* issues that need to be addressed in future studies of nonmaternal infant care, underlying *theoretical* differences continue to affect how data are collected, analyzed, and interpreted. We hope that by explicating these theoretical issues, researchers will be able to design studies that specifically address the mechanisms and processes by which early nonmaternal care affects infant development.

To illustrate the role of theory, we focus specifically on the topic of infant-mother attachment. Nearly all researchers studying the effects of nonmaternal care initiated in the first year of life agree that the quality of the infant's attachment to the mother is an important outcome variable. There are several reasons the primary focus has been on the infant's attachment to the mother. From a larger social perspective, the issue of maternal employment threatens our cultural conceptions of the sanctity of motherhood and the importance of an exclusive child-mother relationship, especially before a child enters school (Hock, DeMeis, and McBride, 1988; McCartney and Phillips, 1988). From several theoretical perspectives, including psychosocial (Erikson, 1963), object relations (Greenberg and Mitchell, 1983) and evolutionary-ethological (Bowlby, 1982), the central developmental task of infancy is the establishment of selective relationships with caregivers. From an empirical perspective, the fact that we have a reliable measure of infant-mother attachment (that is, the Strange Situation Assessment) with some predictive value (for example, Ainsworth, Blehar, Waters, and Wall, 1978; Lamb, 1987; Lamb, Thompson, Gardner, and Charnov, 1985; Sroufe and Waters, 1977) has also contributed to this emphasis.

Researchers are in agreement that nonmaternal infant care does not necessarily prevent the formation of an attachment relationship between mother and infant (Rutter, 1981), but they have increasingly begun to ask whether full-time nonmaternal care initiated in the first year of life can affect the *quality* of the infant-mother relationship. Although researchers have begun to search for variables in the ecology of child care that constitute risk factors for the development of an insecure infant-mother attachment, few have explicitly discussed the processes and mechanisms by which these factors operate (Belsky, in press).

Implicit in this search have been two different perspectives on how the quality of infant-mother attachment can be affected by nonmaternal infant care. In this chapter, we describe these two perspectives, briefly trace their origins, and illustrate how each perspective leads to superficially similar, but fundamentally different, research strategies. Because these models are implicit in the literature, researchers have not explicitly identified with one model or the other. Moreover, because these models are not mutually exclusive, researchers have often adopted complex blends of these models in understanding the complex effects of nonmaternal care. However, by considering these perspectives as separate and distinct models, we hope to facilitate more explicit discussion of these different theoretical assumptions. Such discussion is particularly important as researchers begin using more complex, blended models to explain the effects of early nonmaternal care. After presenting these models, we discuss procedures by which their fundamental assumptions can be tested.

Two Models of the Effects of Nonmaternal Infant Care

Two explanations can be discerned regarding the mechanism by which early nonmaternal care can affect the security of infant-mother attachment. The first type of explanation focuses on the direct impact of separation, inherent in nonmaternal care, on the infant. We call this the *maternal separation model*. The second type of explanation considers the effects of maternal employment on the quality of mother-infant interaction and, in turn, on the security of infant attachment. We call this the *quality of mothering model*.

In the maternal separation model, nonmaternal care is viewed as synonymous with mother-infant separation (see Figure 1). According to this model, the effects of nonmaternal infant care can be attributed to the fact that alternative care is associated with daily, repeated separations from the mother. Researchers using this model argue that infants experiencing daily separations are either likely to interpret maternal absence as rejection (Barglow, Vaughn, and Molitor, 1987; Blehar, 1974; Schwartz, 1983; Vaughn, Gove, and Egeland, 1980) or at least come to doubt maternal availability and responsiveness (Belsky, 1986). Maternal rejection, psychological unavailability, and unresponsiveness have been found to be the antecedents of insecure attachments (Ainsworth, Blehar, Waters, and Wall, 1978). Therefore, child care effects on attachment security are attributed to changes in

Figure 1. Two Explanations of Nonmaternal Care Effects

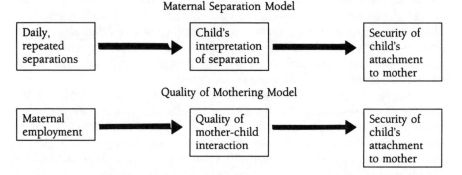

the child's interpretation of the mother's availability. Although home-reared infants come to believe their mothers are unavailable or inaccessible based on the mother's behaviors in the *presence* of the child, infants in nonmaternal care come to believe in the mother's unavailability based on her *absence*. According to the maternal separation model, greater rates of insecure attachment, specifically, avoidance, are predicted for infants experiencing significant nonmaternal care.

The quality of mothering model posits that the effects of maternal employment on the security of infant attachment are indirect, mediated through their effects on the quality of mother-infant interaction (see Figure 1). Researchers within this model argue that it is not maternal employment (or separation) per se that determines infant outcome (Ainslie and Anderson, 1984; Benn, 1986; Chase-Lansdale and Owen, 1987; Goldberg and Easterbrooks, 1988; Goosens, 1987; Hoffman, 1989; Lamb, 1982; Owen and Cox, 1988; Rutter, 1981; Weinraub, Jaeger, and Hoffman, 1988). These researchers instead argue that to understand the effects of maternal employment or nonmaternal care on attachment security, one must consider how maternal employment ultimately affects parental behavior. From this perspective, no predictions are made regarding infant attachment solely on the basis of maternal employment status, because there is no reason to assume a priori that maternal employment status in and of itself affects a mother's parenting behavior. If differences in infant outcome are found, it is presumed that maternal employment status has had some effect on the ecology of the mother-infant dyad that compromises the employed mother's ability to be a sensitive and responsive caregiver.

The empirical roots of these explanations lie in two distinct research traditions. In general, the study of the effects of nonmaternal care on infant development has been approached from two complementary, yet distinct, research perspectives. Some researchers study the effects of day care, while others study the effects of maternal employment. The two research agendas are not synonymous (Lamb, Chase-Lansdale, and Owen, 1979).

Day-care researchers have traditionally been concerned with the direct effects of variables pertaining to the child care setting on infant development. The maternal separation model is consistent with the day-care research tradition because it posits a direct impact of nonmaternal care on infant attachment security. Maternal employment researchers, in contrast, have been concerned with how maternal employment status affects family dynamics, parental care behavior, and, in turn, child development. The quality of mothering model is consistent with this research perspective. Traditionally, researchers from each perspective have acknowledged but rarely measured the influence of variables pertaining to the other perspective. (For a notable exception, see Phillips, McCartney, and Scarr, 1987.)

Today, researchers from both perspectives acknowledge that a comprehensive understanding of the effects of nonmaternal care necessitates consideration of variables relevant to the child care and family settings and an appreciation of their complex interactions. However, it is important to examine separately the two explanations we have identified with each research perspective because as researchers from different traditions come together, each brings to bear a different theoretical perspective and related research strategy.

Theoretical Origins of the Two Models

Both the maternal separation model and the quality of mothering model derive from ethological attachment theory. The similarity of their origins obscures the fact that proponents of each model refer to different, although not necessarily incompatible, aspects of attachment theory. The maternal separation model derives from Bowlby's theoretical and clinical formulations regarding the etiology of insecure attachments. The quality of mothering model, on the other hand, is based on Ainsworth's (see Ainsworth, Blehar, Waters, and Wall, 1978) empirical work examining the antecedents of individual differences in attachment patterns, as assessed in the Strange Situation.

Origins of the Maternal Separation Model. The impetus to the formulation of attachment theory was research examining the responses of children who were separated from their attachment figure. Thus, it is not surprising that Bowlby (1973) attributed a major role to separation experiences in the formation of insecure or anxious attachments. Bowlby maintained that, particularly before the age of three, "separation from mother figure is in itself a key variable determining a child's emotional state and behavior" (1973, p. 22). Only when a child is old enough to represent attachment figures internally is the child able to feel secure in the absence of the mother figure. Early separation experiences are likely to cause an infant to develop internal representations that portray attachment figures as inaccessible. Because these "internal working models," as Bowlby (1973,

1982) called them, influence attachment behavior throughout life, early separations can have a pathogenic influence over the entire course of development.

Bowlby never specified exactly how much (and what kind of) separation an infant can tolerate before there are permanent consequences for the security of infant attachment. He has, however, explicitly stated that full-time day care "is an undesirably stressful experience" (1973, p. 33). Based on Bowlby's (1951, 1973) comments, some researchers have assumed that attachment theory predicts that infants in full-time nonmaternal care are more likely to form insecure attachments.

Another aspect of Bowlby's theory relevant to the issue of nonmaternal care is the concept of monotrophy. Bowlby (1982) believed that the infant is innately *monotrophic,* that is, genetically predisposed to become primarily attached to one figure. Although Bowlby acknowledged that infants can form more than one attachment, he considered these other relationships subsidiary to the primary attachment relationship. Even if infants in child care have formed some sort of subsidiary attachment to an alternative caregiver, this relationship cannot fully compensate for the relationship with the primary attachment figure. It is the separation from the primary attachment figure that may shake the infant's confidence both in the mother's availability and in the infant's ability to elicit care (Sroufe, 1988).

Rutter (1979) has raised concerns regarding Bowlby's emphasis on separation as an etiological factor. Based on more current research on maternal deprivation, Rutter (1979) has concluded that although separation is a stressor, many of the effects attributed to maternal deprivation, such as conduct disorders, are the result of family disturbances that occur prior to the separation. Furthermore, Rutter (1979) has emphasized that research indicates that many children are not adversely affected by separation experiences, and hence separation as such is probably not the mechanism responsible for child outcome. However, although Rutter and other maternal deprivation researchers have examined the effects of separation on a variety of outcomes from personality disturbances to intellectual retardation, they have not examined the impact of separation specifically on the quality of infant attachment. It is possible that the security of infant attachment is more vulnerable to the effects of separation than other outcome measures.

Origins of the Quality of Mothering Model. In their longitudinal investigation of mother-infant interaction over the first year of life, Ainsworth, Blehar, Waters, and Wall (1978) found that secure infants had mothers who were more sensitive to their infant's signals, more cooperative, more psychologically available, and more accepting of their infants than were mothers of insecure infants. More important, qualitative aspects of discrete measures of maternal behavior were more potent predictors of attachment security than simple quantitative measures. For example, *how* a mother held her baby, rather than the *amount of time* she spent holding her baby, was more important in differentiating mothers of secure and insecure infants.

Because Ainsworth, Blehar, Waters, and Wall (1978) examined the antecedents of attachment security only in home-reared infants, their data did not directly address the issue of nonmaternal infant care. Nevertheless, some researchers have generalized their findings to the antecedents of attachment patterns in children of employed mothers. Specifically, researchers have drawn a parallel inference from the research on infant-father attachment, which has shown that infants are as likely to form secure attachments with their fathers as they are with their mothers, despite the fact that infants and fathers are usually separated daily (for example, Lamb, 1978; Main and Weston, 1981). These studies showed that *qualities* of paternal behavior, not *how much time* the father spends with his infant, were important determinants of attachment security (for example, Easterbrooks and Goldberg, 1984; Lamb, 1978). Researchers then interpret these findings to mean that the quality, not quantity, of maternal behavior must also be the primary determinant of attachment security in infants of employed mothers (Clarke-Stewart, 1988).

Using research on infant-father attachment to argue that separation per se is irrelevant in the case of nonmaternal infant care overlooks an important tenet of attachment theory: the importance of a primary attachment figure. Both Bowlby and Ainsworth believe that the infant is monotrophic, with the mother most often serving as the primary attachment figure. Research on infant-father attachment may only be relevant to understanding the nature of subsidiary attachment relationships. The determinants of attachment security in subsidiary attachments may differ from the determinants in primary attachments.

Attachment theory and the research inspired by the theory do not provide the basis for favoring or eliminating either model of the effects of nonmaternal care. Both Bowlby's and Ainsworth's contributions to attachment theory are the product of the types of infants and situations they examined. Bowlby based his conclusions on observations of clinical samples, and hence he came to emphasize the critical role that separation experiences play in the development of insecure attachments. Ainsworth, on the other hand, studied home-reared infants. If quantitative variations in mother-infant interaction do affect attachment security, they probably did not emerge in her research because there was not enough variation in her sample to detect such relationships.

None of the research on which attachment theory is based is directly relevant to the case of employed-mother families, and the basic postulates of attachment theory do not speak directly to the case of employed-mother families (Richters and Zahn-Waxler, 1988). Research on nonmaternal care effects may illuminate how circumstances such as temporary, repeated separations affect infant-mother attachment relationships. In this way, research on the effects of early nonmaternal care may offer important insights regarding the theoretical processes of attachment. Thus, not only does attachment theory have an important function to play in studies of the effects of nonmaternal infant care, but also research on nonmaternal infant care may inform attachment theory.

Research Perspectives: Elaborating the Models

Child care researchers, whether coming from the day-care or the maternal employment research traditions, face the common task of explaining the great variability in outcomes for infants who experience nonmaternal care. Richters and Zahn-Waxler (1988, p. 319) phrase the fundamental research question as, "Under what conditions are what outcomes associated with what patterns of early nonmaternal care, to what extent, and why?" Belsky and Rovine (this volume) conceptualize the research agenda as a search for variables in the ecology of child care that may be risk factors. Depending on their theoretical assumptions, researchers have different strategies for approaching these issues empirically.

Maternal Separation Model. Within the maternal separation model, the search for the basis of individual differences in infant outcomes focuses on variables that are likely to affect the infant's interpretation of maternal absence. If the mechanism by which early nonmaternal care influences attachment security is the infant's interpretation of maternal separation as rejection, then relevant process variables are ones that could influence this interpretation. These moderating variables can be classified into four groups: parameters of the separation, nature of the child's experience during maternal absence, characteristics of the infant, and qualities of the mother-child relationship (see Figure 2).

Separation Parameters. Separations vary across a number of parameters

Figure 2. Maternal Separation Model

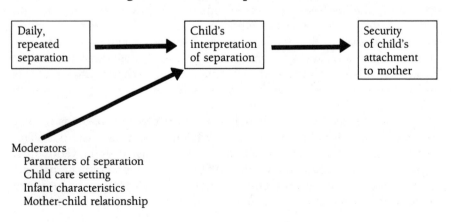

Moderators
Parameters of separation
Child care setting
Infant characteristics
Mother-child relationship

that can affect how an infant interprets separation. Bowlby (1973) suggested that the *length* of separation is important in determining the child's response. In child care research, this issue has been globally examined by comparing infants in full-time versus part-time nonmaternal care (Barglow, Vaughn, and Molitor, 1987; Belsky and Rovine, 1988; Goldberg and Easterbrooks, 1988; Owen and Cox, 1988). Another aspect of separations is the *frequency* with which they occur. Bowlby (1973) suggested that the repetition of separation experience, regardless of length, can affect outcome adversely. In addition, the *predictability* of the separation can influence outcome, with predictable separations being less stressful (Ainsworth, Blehar, Waters, and Wall, 1978; Bowlby, 1973).

Infant's Experience During the Separation. Both Bowlby (1973) and Ainsworth, Blehar, Waters, and Wall (1978) emphasized the critical role that alternative care arrangements play in moderating responses to separation. In particular, they emphasized two features: the *continuity* of the caregiving arrangements and the *sensitivity* of the alternative caregivers. Although researchers have begun to examine the impact of the stability of the caregiving arrangements on attachment security (Belsky and Rovine, 1988; Benn, 1986; Goldberg and Easterbrooks, 1988), the relationship between alternative caregiver sensitivity and infant-mother attachment has not yet been addressed. Some researchers have examined the impact on child attachment security of different types of alternate care (Belsky and Rovine, 1988; Benn, 1986; Weinraub and Jaeger, in press), but they have not specifically addressed how type of care correlates with quality of the infant-caregiver relationship.

From the standpoint of attachment theory, the quality of caregiver-infant attachment may be the most critical variable to examine. If the child has formed a secure attachment to an alternative caregiver, the separation from the mother may be less stressful. In addition, if the child becomes stressed during maternal absence and attachment behavior becomes activated, a sensitive caregiver to whom an infant is attached can be used as a secure base. If the infant's attachment behaviors are adequately responded to by the alternate caregiver during maternal absence, it is less likely the infant will evoke defensive processes to cope with maternal separation. Researchers are beginning to examine directly the quality of infant-caregiver attachment (Howes, Rodning, Galluzzo, and Myers, 1988), but the effects of this relationship on infant-mother attachment are not yet fully understood.

Infant Characteristics. Individual differences with respect to separation distress can also influence an infant's interpretation of the separation experience. Three variables have been considered by researchers: gender, temperament, and child's age at onset of nonmaternal care. The influence of gender has been considered because males tend to be more stressed by separation than females (Aisenstein and Weinraub, 1989; Belsky and

Rovine, 1988; DiBiase, Weinraub, Ansul, and Jaeger, 1988; Weinraub and Frankel, 1977; Weinraub and Lewis, 1977). Infant temperament has been suggested as a potential moderator of nonmaternal care effects (Belsky and Rovine, 1988; Benn, 1986; Gamble and Zigler, 1986; Kagan, Kearsley, and Zelaso, 1978; Rutter, 1981).

The infant's age at the onset of nonmaternal care may also be a potential moderator of nonmaternal care effects. Both Ainsworth, Blehar, Waters, and Wall (1978) and Hoffman (1984) have suggested that nonmaternal care initiated prior to six months of age, that is, prior to the consolidation of the infant-mother attachment relationship, may be less stressful than care initiated later in the first year of life. This is because the initiation of nonmaternal care during the period of time that the infant-mother attachment is becoming consolidated—eight to twelve months after birth—may be particularly distressing insofar as it violates the expectations the infant has begun to develop regarding the mother's availability. (For further discussion of this issue, see Weinraub and Jaeger, in press.) In addition, it is during this time that separation distress and stranger anxiety emerge. Therefore, according to this view, the infant may be particularly likely to interpret maternal absence as rejection if nonmaternal care is initiated *later,* rather than earlier, in the first year of life.

Qualities of the Mother-Child Relationship. Within the maternal separation model, the quality of mother-child interaction may be seen as a moderator of the effects of nonmaternal care, determining the extent to which nonmaternal care has a negative impact on attachment security. Separation is still assumed to have a direct, negative effect on attachment security, but this effect may be buffered by high-quality maternal care. For infants who experience very positive interactions with their mothers, the infant's interpretation of maternal absence as rejection may be counterbalanced by the infant's more enduring belief in the mother's otherwise great availability and responsivity. Similarly, when the quality of the mother-child relationship is poor, the infant may be even more likely to interpret maternal absence as rejection.

Quality of Mothering Model. From the perspective of the quality of mothering model, the effects of nonmaternal care on the security of infant-mother attachment are mediated by the quality of mother-infant interaction. In this model, it is assumed that nonmaternal care, and any other variables relating to maternal employment, affect child attachment security by way of their effects on the qualities of mother-infant interaction. Here, qualities of the mother-child relationship are not simply moderators of the effects of nonmaternal care, determining to what extent nonmaternal care may influence the child's interpretation of the separation and hence his or her attachment security. Rather, qualities of the mother-child interaction mediate the effects of maternal employment. That is, they are the mechanism by which characteristics of nonmaternal care and maternal employment are effective. If any effects of nonmaternal care or maternal employment status on attachment security are noted, these are understood, according to this model, by examining how variables associated with nonmaternal care and maternal employment affect the mother-child interaction.

In essence, the quality of mothering model is a specific example of the process models researchers have used to understand infant outcomes in families regardless of nonmaternal care status (for example, Belsky, 1984). Some researchers (for example, Lerner and Galambos, 1988; Richters and Zahn-Waxler, 1988) have already begun to elaborate the model for families using nonmaternal infant care. Here, we describe the types of variables researchers have considered, suggest some new ones, and discuss how these are interpreted from the framework of the quality of mothering model. Particularly relevant variables can be categorized as follows: the quality of the mother's life, family dynamics, and maternal attitudes and personality characteristics (see Figure 3).

Quality of the Mother's Life. Perhaps the most important indicator of the quality of a mother's life is her sense of satisfaction with her various roles. Early findings suggested that role satisfaction, regardless of maternal employment status, is a better predictor of child outcome than employment status (Hoffman, 1961; Yarrow, Scott, DeLeeuw, and Heinig, 1962). Maternal role satisfaction, and alternatively role conflict, can affect the mother's ability to be sensitive and responsive and thereby affect attachment security (Lerner and Galambos, 1988). Although role satisfaction has been shown to be related to qualities of mother-infant interaction (Stuckey, McGhee, and Bell, 1982) and also to infant attachment behavior in the Strange Situation for families of employed mothers (Hock, 1980; Jaeger, Weinraub, Becker,

Figure 3. Quality of Mothering Model

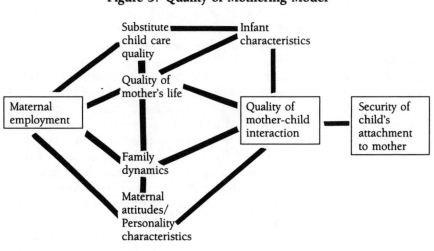

and Jaeger, 1989), it still remains to be demonstrated within a single study that role satisfaction affects mother-infant interaction, which then affects attachment security.

Sources of stress and support that can contribute to a mother's overall sense of satisfaction are also important from this perspective. To what extent does a mother's employment status or choice of child care status represent a source of stress or support? It is possible that these factors influence the mother's parenting behavior independently of the mother's perceived role satisfaction.

Family Dynamics. Although most child care research has focused on the mother-infant dyad, the entire family system affects and is affected by the decision to use nonmaternal care. The role of the father may be critical in dual-earner families. The father's participation in caregiving and household responsibilities, as well as his role as an emotional support for the mother, may directly influence the mother's ability to be a sensitive caregiver. In addition, the emotional and practical support he provides may influence marital adjustment (O'Brien and Weinraub, 1987), indirectly influencing maternal behavior and, subsequently, infant attachment (Owen and Cox, 1988). Lower marital satisfaction, as reported by employed mothers, has been found to be associated with greater rates of insecure attachment (Belsky and Rovine, 1988). Similarly, lower family cohesion in families using full-time infant day care is associated with greater rates of infant insecurity (Ainslie, 1987). Extensive use of nonmaternal care in the first year postpartum has also been linked to decreased marital satisfaction (Owen and Cox, 1990) and greater marital conflict (Belsky, in press).

Maternal Attitudes and Personality Characteristics. Within the quality of mothering model, maternal attitudes and personality characteristics may also influence how maternal employment affects parenting behavior. Such factors have already been found to be related to infant outcome in families of employed mothers (Belsky and Rovine, 1988; Benn, 1986; Farber and Egeland, 1982). Within this model, it is important to document that these personality variables function through their effects on the quality of parenting.

Before turning to a discussion of the points of similarity between the two models, three important features of the quality of mothering model should be emphasized. First, the paths of influence among ecological factors such as maternal role satisfaction, marital adjustment, and stress and support are bidirectional. Second, it is unlikely that any of these variables act in isolation. To understand fully the process by which any of these variables can influence mother-infant interaction, one must take into account their complex interactive effects (Richters and Zahn-Waxler, 1988). Third, from the perspective of the quality of mothering model, all variables that can affect parenting behavior must be ruled out as preselection factors before the influence of maternal employment status can be discerned.

Examples of Overlap. In our discussion of the quality of mothering model, the variables we have described thus far would be difficult to interpret from the perspective of the maternal separation model. None of these variables would seem to influence directly the infant's interpretation of maternal absence. We did, however, leave out three variables that the quality of mothering model shares with the maternal separation model (see Figure 3). Specifically, these are the nature of the alternative caregiving arrangements, the infant's temperament, and the infant's age at onset of nonmaternal care. The inclusion of these variables in both models may obscure the fact that the interpretation of each differs in the two models.

From the perspective of the quality of mothering model, the nature of the alternative caregiving arrangements may moderate the effects of maternal employment on the quality of mother-infant interaction and hence affect attachment security. For example, poor child care may be a stress on the mother and thereby compromise her ability to be a responsive parent. Alternatively, good-quality nonmaternal infant care may be a source of support for a mother who feels ambivalent about leaving her infant in nonmaternal care. Changes in the infant's behavior as a result of nonmaternal care may also affect the quality of mother-infant interaction and hence attachment security. Although numerous paths of influence are possible, the quality of mothering model interprets the influence of these child care variables on attachment security as indirect, such that they are mediated by the quality of mother-infant interaction. In the maternal separation model, the effects of alternate care variables are seen as having a more direct impact on infant attachment security, not mediated by the quality of mother-infant interaction, by affecting the infant's interpretation of maternal absence. With adequate longitudinal data, these different interpretations can be tested.

In both models, infant temperament is viewed as important. In the quality of mothering model, infant temperament is viewed as moderating the influence of maternal employment status on mother-infant interaction. For example, a difficult infant may challenge an overloaded mother's ability to be sensitive and responsive. From the standpoint of the maternal separation model, infant temperament may moderate the infant's interpretation of maternal absence, with more irritable infants being generally more distressed in the mother's absence.

Infant age at the onset of nonmaternal care is a third moderating variable relevant to both models. Here the models appear to make opposite predictions regarding the optimal time to initiate nonmaternal care. Reflecting the assumptions of the quality of mothering model, Brazelton (1985) has argued that the onset of nonmaternal care later in the first year of life is preferable to earlier in the first year because it allows the mother greater opportunities to get to know her infant and thereby allows her to become a more sensitive and responsive caregiver. Conversely, on the basis of the maternal separation model, Ainsworth, Blehar, Waters, and Wall (1978) and Hoffman (1984) have argued that nonmaternal care initiated earlier rather than later in the first year may be optimal. The infant may be more likely to interpret maternal absence as rejection of initiation if nonmaternal care is simultaneous with or subsequent to the consolidation of the attachment relationship than if regular, repeated separations precede the consolidation of attachment.

Although it appears that each model predicts different ages to be optimal for initiating nonmaternal care, each model can accommodate results in either direction. If earlier onset of nonmaternal care is associated with better attachment outcomes, supporters of the quality of mothering model can argue that early return to employment is more desirable for some employed mothers and that, consequently ,they can be more sensitive and responsive to their infants. Likewise, if later onset is associated with a better outcome, supporters of the maternal separation model can argue that a delayed onset allows the infant to develop greater confidence in the mother's dependability and hence greater toleration of separation (Sroufe, 1988). Again, it is the interpretation of results that differentiates the two models.

Testing the Models

The critical difference between the two models is whether attachment security is *directly* affected by the experience of nonmaternal care, as predicted by the maternal separation model, or whether the effects of these variables are *mediated* through changes in the quality of the mother-infant interaction, as predicted by the quality of mothering model. Support for either model, therefore, depends on the relationship between the quality of mother-infant interaction and attachment security. If the maternal separation model is correct, characteristics of the nonmaternal care situation, such as the quality and stability of care, should directly predict the child's attachment to the mother. It also follows from this model that the quality of mother-infant interaction should be more strongly related to attachment security in infants of nonemployed mothers than in infants of employed mothers. If the quality of mothering model is correct, when differences between children of employed and nonemployed mothers are found, so also should differences in the quality of mother-infant interaction be found. The quality of mother-infant interaction should be equally predictive of infant attachment in both types of families. Furthermore, any effects of nonmaternal care or maternal employment should be indirect, such that they are mediated through mother-child interaction.

To adequately test these models, at least four requirements must be met in the research design. First, it cannot be emphasized strongly enough that without a reliable measure of mother-infant interaction, *neither* model can be adequately tested. Without such a measure, researchers will be biased toward acceptance of the nonmediated maternal separation model

(Baron and Kenny, 1986). Furthermore, the best support for the maternal separation model entails showing that the quality of mother-infant interaction is *not* a strong predictor of attachment outcome in families using nonmaternal care and that the effects of nonmaternal care variables are *not* mediated by the quality of mother-infant interaction. Likewise, the strongest support for the quality of mothering model depends on showing that the quality of mother-infant interaction is the best predictor of attachment outcome even in families using nonmaternal care and that the effects of nonmaternal care and maternal employment variables are mediated by the quality of mother-infant interaction. Adequate testing of these models demands greater consideration be given to developing reliable and valid measures of mother-infant interaction in future child care research.

Second, to understand fully the process by which either mechanism is influenced by nonmaternal care, researchers must examine the wide range of ecological variables concurrently comprising the family and child care contexts. As we have seen in previous research on nonmaternal infant care, the effects of the same variable can be interpreted differently depending on theoretical assumptions. Therefore, these relevant variables must be assessed simultaneously, and the proposed process by which they relate to attachment outcome must be empirically tested.

Third, adequate testing of these models requires structural modeling techniques. Given the number of variables that must be considered, larger samples of families than have been seen in previous research are required.

Fourth, longitudinal data are necessary so that causal relationships can be determined. Without such data, theoretical assumptions will fully determine how results are interpreted. For example, a concurrent correlation between quality of mother-infant interaction and maternal role satisfaction may mean that a satisfied mother interacts more sensitively with her infant, or, in contrast, it may mean that a mother's role satisfaction is in part determined by how she interacts with her child.

Most maternal employment and child care researchers now agree that to understand fully the consequences of nonmaternal care and maternal employment on infants, we need to capture in our research designs the complex ecology of human development. The collaborative, national study funded by the National Institute of Child Health and Human Development will be able to collect these necessary data (Friedman, 1990). Because theoretical assumptions will influence how these data are collected, analyzed, and interpreted, considerable attention must also be paid to the theory underlying the research questions.

A Caveat

In this chapter, we have considered one outcome variable, the security of infant attachment, which is of interest in the study of the effects of nonmaternal care. The specific models that we have identified here are relevant only to attachment outcome. If the outcome variables of interest are compliance, aggression, or peer relations, for example, the models researchers use to explain the mechanism by which nonmaternal care could affect these outcomes may be different from the ones presented here. However, by using attachment outcome as an example, we hope we have demonstrated the value of considering the theory underlying research hypotheses when designing methods to investigate the effects of nonmaternal care. By explicitly considering theory, current empirical controversies may be exposed as fundamentally theoretical in nature, amenable to explicit testing.

Summary and Conclusion

As day-care researchers and maternal employment researchers join together to study the effects of nonmaternal care, they bring with them different theoretical models concerning how nonmaternal care can affect the security of infant-mother attachment. Because both the maternal separation model and the quality of mothering model derive from attachment theory, fundamental theoretical differences among researchers have been obscured. Although researchers from both models propose that similar variables moderate the effects of nonmaternal care on infant attachment, the models offer different ways of interpreting the meaning of these relationships.

Certainly, blends of these two models have been proposed. For example, Sroufe (1988, p. 286) has hypothesized that "separation and the insecurity it engenders may well leave the young infant more needy of responsive care and at the same time tax the infant-caregiver interactive system. To this is added the caregiver's own anxiety concerning separations and the reduced opportunities for interaction." In this blended model, increased separation distress and less sensitive mother-infant interaction result from nonmaternal care, with each variable moderating the other's effects. Increasingly, researchers are moving toward such blended models as they begin to appreciate the complex ecology of child care.

The new zeitgeist in research examining the effects of nonmaternal care is a deeper appreciation of the great variability in child care environments, both inside and outside of the home. By relying on theory to guide us in the generation of specific empirical hypotheses about how early nonmaternal care can influence our outcome variable of choice, and by being sensitive to differing theoretical predictions concerning the relationships among these variables, researchers may be able to specify the complex interrelated processes underlying the effects of early nonmaternal care.

References

Ainslie, R. C. "The Social Ecology of Day Care Children with Secure and Insecure Maternal Attachments." Paper presented at the annual meeting of the American Psychological Association, New York City, August 28, 1987.

Ainslie, R. C., and Anderson, C. W. "Day Care Children's Relationships to Their Mothers and Caregivers: An Inquiry into the Conditions for the Development of Attachment." In R. C. Ainslie (ed.), *The Child and the Day Care Setting: Qualitative Variations and Development.* New York: Praeger, 1984.

Ainsworth, M.D.S., Blehar, M. C., Waters, E., and Wall, S. *Patterns of Attachment: A Psychological Study of the Strange Situation.* New York: Wiley, 1978.

Aisenstein, J., and Weinraub, M. "Maternal Departure Style and Children's Responses: Is There a Relationship?" Unpublished manuscript, Department of Psychology, Temple University, 1989.

Barglow, P., Vaughn, B. E., and Molitor, N. "Effects of Maternal Absence Due to Employment on the Quality of Infant-Mother Attachment in a Low-Risk Sample." *Child Development,* 1987, 58 (4), 945–954.

Baron, R. M., and Kenny, D. "The Moderator-Mediator Variable Distinction in Social Psychological Research: Conceptual, Strategic, and Statistical Considerations." *Journal of Personality and Social Psychology,* 1986, 51 (6), 1173–1182.

Belsky, J. "The Determinants of Parenting: A Process Model." *Child Development,* 1984, 55 (1), 83–96.

Belsky, J. "Infant Day Care: A Cause for Concern." *Zero to Three,* 1986, 6 (5), 1–7.

Belsky, J. "Parental and Nonparental Child Care and Children's Socioemotional Development." *Journal of Marriage and the Family,* in press.

Belsky, J., and Rovine, M. "Nonmaternal Care in the First Year of Life and the Security of Infant-Parent Attachment." *Child Development,* 1988, 59 (1), 157–167.

Benn, R. K. "Factors Promoting Secure Attachment Relationships Between Employed Mothers and Their Sons." *Child Development,* 1986, 57 (5), 1224–1231.

Blehar, M. C. "Anxious Attachment and Defensive Reactions Associated with Day Care." *Child Development,* 1974, 45 (3), 683–692.

Bowlby, J. *Maternal Care and Mental Health.* Geneva: World Health Organization, 1951.

Bowlby, J. *Attachment and Loss.* Vol. 2: *Separation.* New York: Basic Books, 1973.

Bowlby, J. *Attachment and Loss.* Vol. 1: *Attachment.* (2nd ed.) New York: Basic Books, 1982.

Brazelton, T. B. *Working and Caring.* New York: Basic Books, 1985.

Chase-Lansdale, P. L., and Owen, M. T. "Maternal Employment in a Family Context: Effects on Infant-Mother and Infant-Father Attachments." *Child Development,* 1987, 58 (6), 1505–1512.

Clarke-Stewart, K. A. " 'The "Effects" of Infant Day Care Reconsidered' Reconsidered: Risks for Parents, Children, and Researchers." *Early Childhood Research Quarterly,* 1988, 3 (3), 293–318.

DiBiase, R., Weinraub, M., Ansul, S., and Jaeger, E. "Two Measures of Attachment: Their Relationship to Home Behavior in Infants of Employed and Non-Employed Mothers." Poster presented at the biennial International Conference on Infant Studies, Washington, D.C., 1988.

Easterbrooks, M. A., and Goldberg, W. A. "Toddler Development in the Family: Impact of Father Involvement and Parenting Characteristics." *Child Development,* 1984, 55 (3), 740–752.

Erikson, E. H. *Childhood and Society.* New York: Norton, 1963.

Farber, E. A., and Egeland, B. "Developmental Consequences of Out-of-Home Care for Infants in a Low-Income Population." In E. F. Zigler and E. W. Gordon (eds.), *Day Care: Scientific and Social Policy Issues.* Boston: Auburn House, 1982.

Friedman, S. "NICHD Infant Child-Care Network: The National Study of Young Children's Lives." *Zero to Three,* 1990, 10 (3), 21–23.

Gamble, T. J., and Zigler, E. "Effects of Infant Day Care: Another Look at the Evidence." *American Journal of Orthopsychiatry,* 1986, 56 (1), 26–42.

Goldberg, W. A., and Easterbrooks, M. A. "Maternal Employment When Children Are Toddlers and Kindergartners." In A. E. Gottfried and A. W. Gottfried (eds.), *Maternal Employment and Children's Development: Longitudinal Research.* New York: Plenum, 1988.

Goosens, F. A. "Maternal Employment and Day Care: Effects on Attachment." In L.W.C. Tavecchio and M. H. Van Ijzendoorn (eds.), *Attachment in Social Networks.* Amsterdam: North-Holland, 1987.

Greenberg, J. R., and Mitchell, S. A. *Object Relations and Psychoanalytic Theory.* Cambridge, Mass.: Harvard University Press, 1983.

Hock, E. "Working and Nonworking Mothers and Their Infants: A Comparative Study of Maternal Caregiving Characteristics and Infant Social Behavior." *Merrill-Palmer Quarterly,* 1980, *26* (2), 79–101.

Hock, E., DeMeis, D., and McBride, S. "Maternal Separation Anxiety: Its Role in the Balance of Employment and Motherhood in Mothers of Infants." In A. E. Gottfried and A. W. Gottfried (eds.), *Maternal Employment and Children's Development: Longitudinal Research.* New York: Plenum, 1988.

Hoffman, L. W. "The Effects of Maternal Employment on the Child." *Child Development,* 1961, *32* (1), 187–197.

Hoffman, L. W. "Maternal Employment and the Young Child." In M. Perlmutter (ed.), *Parent-Child Interaction.* Minnesota Symposium Series, no. 17. Hillsdale, N.J.: Erlbaum, 1984.

Hoffman, L. W. "Effects of Maternal Employment in the Two-Parent Family." *American Psychologist,* 1989, *44* (2), 283–292.

Howes, C., Rodning, C., Galluzzo, D. C., and Myers, L. "Attachment and Child Care: Relationships with Mother and Caregiver." *Early Childhood Research Quarterly,* 1988, *3* (4), 403–416.

Jaeger, E., Weinraub, M., Becker, N., and Jaeger, M. "Attachment, Dependency, and Separation Distress in Infants of Employed Mothers." Poster presented at the biennial meeting of the Society for Research in Child Development, Kansas City, Missouri, April 1989.

Kagan, J., Kearsley, R. B., and Zelaso, P. R. *Infancy: Its Place in Human Development.* Cambridge, Mass.: Harvard University Press, 1978.

Lamb, M. E. "Qualitative Aspects of Mother- and Father-Infant Attachments." *Infant Behavior and Development,* 1978, *1* (3), 265–275.

Lamb, M. E. "Maternal Employment and Child Development: A Review." In M. E. Lamb (ed.), *Nontraditional Families: Parenting and Child Development.* Hillsdale, N.J.: Erlbaum, 1982.

Lamb, M. E. "Predictive Implications of Individual Differences in Attachment." *Journal of Consulting and Clinical Psychology,* 1987, *55* (6), 817–824.

Lamb, M., Chase-Lansdale, L., and Owen, M. "The Changing American Family and Its Implications for Infant Social Development: The Sample Case of Maternal Employment." In M. Lewis and L. A. Rosenblum (eds.), *The Child and Its Family.* New York: Plenum, 1979.

Lamb, M. E., Thompson, R. A., Gardner, W. P., and Charnov, E. L. *Infant-Mother Attachment: The Origins and Developmental Significance of Individual Differences in Strange Situation Behavior.* Hillsdale, N.J.: Erlbaum, 1985.

Lerner, J., and Galambos, N. "The Influence of Maternal Employment Across Life: The New York Longitudinal Study." In A. E. Gottfried and A. W. Gottfried (eds.), *Maternal Employment and Children's Development: Longitudinal Research.* New York: Plenum, 1988.

McCartney, K., and Phillips, D. "Motherhood and Child Care." In B. Birns and D. Hay (eds.), *Different Faces of Motherhood.* New York: Plenum, 1988.

McCartney, K., Scarr, S., Phillips, D., Grajek, S., and Schwarz, J. C. "Environmental

Differences Among Day Care Centers and Their Effects on Children's Development." In E. F. Zigler and E. W. Gordon (eds.), *Day Care: Scientific and Social Policy Issues.* Boston: Auburn House, 1982.

Main, M., and Weston, D. R. "The Quality of the Toddler's Relationship to Mother and Father: Related to Conflict Behavior and the Readiness to Establish New Relationships." *Child Development,* 1981, 52 (3), 932–940.

National Center for Clinical Infant Programs. *Infants, Families, and Child Care: Toward a Research Agenda.* Washington, D.C.: National Center for Clinical Infant Programs, 1988.

O'Brien, M., and Weinraub, M. "Father Support and Marital Adjustment in Families with Employed and Nonemployed Mothers." Unpublished manuscript, Department of Psychology, Temple University, 1987.

Owen, M. T., and Cox, M. J. "Maternal Employment and the Transition to Parenthood." In A. E. Gottfried and A. W. Gottfried (eds.), *Maternal Employment and Children's Development: Longitudinal Research.* New York: Plenum, 1988.

Owen, M. T., and Cox, M. J. "Maternal Employment and Marital Quality During the First Year of Parenthood." Paper presented at the seventh International Conference on Infant Studies, Montreal, Quebec, April 1990.

Phillips, D., McCartney, K., and Scarr, S. "Child-Care Quality and Children's Social Development." *Developmental Psychology,* 1987, 23 (4), 537–543.

Phillips, D., McCartney, K., Scarr, S., and Howes, C. "Selective Review of Infant Day Care Research: A Cause for Concern." *Zero to Three,* 1987, 7 (3), 18–21.

Richters, J. E., and Zahn-Waxler, C. "The Infant Day Care Controversy: Current Status and Future Directions." *Early Childhood Research Quarterly,* 1988, 3 (3), 319–336.

Rutter, M. "Maternal Deprivation, 1972–1978: New Findings, New Concepts, New Approaches." *Child Development,* 1979, 50 (2), 283–305.

Rutter, M. "Social-Emotional Consequences of Day Care for Preschool Children." *American Journal of Orthopsychiatry,* 1981, 51 (1), 4–28.

Schwartz, P. "Length of Day-Care Attendance and Behavior in Eighteen-Month-Old Infants." *Child Development,* 1983, 54 (4), 1073–1078.

Sroufe, A. L. "A Developmental Perspective on Day Care." *Early Childhood Research Quarterly,* 1988, 3 (3), 283–291.

Sroufe, A. L., and Waters, E. "Attachment as an Organizational Construct." *Child Development,* 1977, 48 (4), 1184–1199.

Stuckey, M. F., McGhee, P. E., and Bell, N. J. "Parent-Child Interaction: The Influence of Maternal Employment." *Developmental Psychology,* 1982, 18, 635–644.

Thompson, R. A. "The Effects of Infant Day Care Through the Prism of Attachment Theory: A Critical Appraisal." *Early Childhood Research Quarterly,* 1988, 3 (3), 273–282.

Vaughn, B. E., Gove, F. L., and Egeland, B. "The Relationship Between Out-of-Home Care and the Quality of Infant-Mother Attachment in an Economically Disadvantaged Population." *Child Development,* 1980, 51 (4), 1203–1214.

Weinraub, M., and Frankel, J. "Sex Differences in Parent-Infant Interaction During Free-Play, Separations, and Reunion." *Child Development,* 1977, 48 (4), 1240–1249.

Weinraub, M., and Jaeger, E. "When Mothers Return to the Workplace: Effects on the Developing Mother-Infant Relationship." In J. S. Hyde and M. J. Essex (eds.), *Parental Leave and Child Care: Setting a Research and Policy Agenda.* Philadelphia: Temple University Press, in press.

Weinraub, M., Jaeger, E., and Hoffman, L. "Predicting Infant Outcomes in Families of Employed and Nonemployed Mothers." *Early Childhood Research Quarterly,* 1988, 3 (4), 361–378,

Weinraub, M., and Lewis, M. *The Determinants of Children's Responses to Separation.* Monographs of the Society for Research in Child Development, vol. 42, no. 4 (serial no. 172). Chicago: University of Chicago Press, 1977.

Yarrow, M. R., Scott, P., DeLeeuw, L., and Heinig, C. "Childrearing in Families of Working and Non-Working Mothers." *Sociometry,* 1962, 25, 122–140.

Elizabeth Jaeger is an advanced doctoral student in developmental psychology at Temple University, Philadelphia.

Marsha Weinraub is a professor of psychology at Temple University, Philadelphia.

INDEX

Aber, J. L., 58, 69
After-school care, 30, 31
Age, of children, at entry into day care, 2, 8, 9, 40, 80, 83-84
Aggression, development of, 7, 8, 9, 18
Ainslie, R. C., 3, 20, 21, 48, 50, 74, 82, 86, 87
Ainsworth, M.D.S., 7, 21, 42, 45, 50, 51, 72, 74, 75, 76-77, 79, 80, 83, 87
Aisenstein, J., 79, 87
Ambron, S. R., 41, 49, 51, 53, 69
Anderson, C. W., 48, 50, 74, 87
Andersson, B. E., 9, 21, 25, 36
ANOVA, 28, 29
Ansul, S., 79, 87
Arnett, J., 63, 69
Attachment Q-Sort, 10-20
Attachment security, 8, 9; and early non-maternal care, 71-86; factors in, 39-50; measures of, 4, 10-20, 42-43, 77

Barglow, P., 4, 5, 11, 21, 50, 51, 74, 79, 87
Baron, R. M., 84, 87
Becker, M., 81, 88
Bell, N. J., 81, 89
Belsky, J., 3, 4, 5, 7, 8, 9, 10, 11, 12, 15, 17, 18, 20, 21, 23, 25, 26, 36, 41, 51, 55, 56, 58, 68, 70, 71, 73, 74, 78, 79-80, 81, 82, 87
Benedek, T., 54, 58, 69
Benn, R. K., 20, 21, 41, 48, 51, 74, 79, 80, 82, 87
Berger, B., 58, 69
Bergman, A., 54, 70
Bermuda Day Care Study, 3
Birth order, 2, 30, 31, 43
Blehar, M. C., 42, 45, 50, 51, 72, 74, 75, 76-77, 79, 80, 83, 87
Bookstein, F. L., 6, 37
Bowlby, J., 54, 69, 72, 75, 76, 77, 78, 87
Brainerd, C. J., 15, 22
Brazelton, T. B., 83, 87
Broberg, A., 6, 37
Bronfenbrenner, U., 1, 4, 5

Cain, R. L., 41, 52
Campbell, F. A., 4, 6

Caregiver Interaction Scale, 63, 68
Caregivers: and infant attachment, 39-40, 42-45, 48; qualifications of, 24-25
Carolina Abecedarian Project, 4-5
Charnov, E. L., 72, 88
Chase-Lansdale, P. L., 26, 36, 74, 87, 88
Child care, and child development, 28-35, 39-42; explanations of, 73-78
Child care environments, variations in, 24-25, 40. See also Day care
Child care research: and research design, 84-86; theoretical issues in, 72-73, 75-84
Clarke-Stewart, K. A., 4, 5, 7, 10, 18, 19, 20, 21, 23, 25, 36, 50, 51, 77, 87
Cleminshaw, H., 46, 51
Cleminshaw-Guidubaldi Parent Satisfaction Scale, 46
Clifford, R. M., 63, 69
Coelen, C., 24, 37
Cognitive Abilities Test, 27, 29, 32, 33
Comprehensive Test of Basic Skills (CTBS), 27, 29, 31, 32
Consortium for Longitudinal Studies, 23, 36
Corasaniti, M. A., 3, 4, 8, 9, 69
Cox, M. J., 26-27, 37, 74, 79, 82, 89
Cummings, E. M., 48, 51

Davis, A. J., 40, 41, 51
Day care: extent of, 8, 9; parental contact with, 44-45, 48; quality of, 2, 3, 9, 63, 64-65, 83; variables of, 42-45. See also Child care
Deane, K. E., 6, 10, 12, 22
DeLeeuw, L., 81, 90
DeMeis, D. K., 3, 5, 25, 36, 53, 55, 56, 67, 69, 72, 88
Demographic variables, 18
Dependency, of child, 11, 12-13. See also Attachment security
DiBiase, R., 79, 87
Duncan post hoc analyses, 28
Dyadic Adjustment Scale, 46

Early Childhood Environmental Rating Scale (ECERS), 63, 65, 68

Ordering Information

NEW DIRECTIONS FOR CHILD DEVELOPMENT is a series of paperback books that presents the latest research findings on all aspects of children's psychological development, including their cognitive, social, moral, and emotional growth. Books in the series are published quarterly in Fall, Winter, Spring, and Summer and are available for purchase by subscription as well as by single copy.

SUBSCRIPTIONS for 1990 cost $48.00 for individuals (a savings of 20 percent over single-copy prices) and $70.00 for institutions, agencies, and libraries. Please do not send institutional checks for personal subscriptions. Standing orders are accepted.

SINGLE COPIES cost $15.95 when payment accompanies order. (California, New Jersey, New York, and Washington, D.C., residents please include appropriate sales tax.) Billed orders will be charged postage and handling.

DISCOUNTS FOR QUANTITY ORDERS are available. Please write to the address below for information.

ALL ORDERS must include either the name of an individual or an official purchase order number. Please submit your order as follows:
   Subscriptions: specify series and year subscription is to begin
   Single copies: include individual title code (such as CD1)

MAIL ALL ORDERS TO:
   Jossey-Bass Inc., Publishers
   350 Sansome Street
   San Francisco, California 94104

FOR SALES OUTSIDE OF THE UNITED STATES CONTACT:
   Maxwell Macmillan International Publishing Group
   866 Third Avenue
   New York, New York 10022

OTHER TITLES AVAILABLE IN THE
NEW DIRECTIONS FOR CHILD DEVELOPMENT SERIES
William Damon, Editor-in-Chief